HEAVEN
A PLACE, A CITY, A HOME

HEAVEN

A PLACE, A CITY, A HOME

EDWARD M. BOUNDS

BAKER BOOK HOUSE
Grand Rapids, Michigan

Paperback edition issued 1975
by Baker Book House

ISBN: 0-8010-0648-1

First printing, October 1975
Second printing, April 1976
Third printing, October 1978
Fourth printing, January 1983

Printed in the United States of America

Introduction

EDWARD McKENDRIE BOUNDS was
born in Shelby County, Mo., August 15,
1835, and died August 24, 1913, in Washington, Ga. He was admitted to the bar, but was
called into the Civil War as chaplain of the Fifth
Missouri Regiment, too early to practice law.

He married Miss Emmie Barnett of Eufaula,
Ala., in 1876. By this union he became the father
of two daughters, Mrs. Bounds Ficklin and Mrs.
Bounds Barnett. His wife died in 1886, and later
he was married to Miss .Hattie Barnett, by whom
he became the father of five children, Miss Elizabeth Bounds, Miss Mary Willis and Miss Emmie,
Osborn and Barnett. All his children are living.

After serving several important churches in St.
Louis and other places, south, he became Editor
of the *St. Louis Christian Advocate* for eight years
and, later, Associate Editor of *The Nashville
Christian Advocate* for four years. The trial of
his faith came to him while in Nashville, and he
quietly retired to his home without asking even a
pension. His principal work in Washington,
Ga. (his home) was rising at 4 A. M. and praying until 7 A. M. He filled a few engagements as

an evangelist during the eighteen years of his life-work in Washington, Ga.

While pastor in Atlanta, in 1905, the writer was informed that there was an apostolic man of prayer in Georgia that would aid the church in attaining a high altitude in spiritual things. The next mail carried a letter asking Mr. Bounds to come to our Convention for ten days' preaching. Naturally we expected to see a man of imposing physique, but when he came we discovered that he was only about five and a half feet tall, but in him we met one of the greatest saints that, in our humble opinion, has appeared on the spiritual horizon in the last hundred years.

He spoke the first afternoon on Prayer. No one seemed to be particularly impressed. The next morning at 4 A. M. we were amazed to hear him engaged in the most wonderful prayer we have ever listened to—a prayer that seemed to take in both Heaven and Earth. His sermons were all about *Prayer and Heaven*. Not one morning during his stay did he fail to make his prayers at the " Great-While-Before-Day " Hour. He cared nothing for the protests of the other occupants of his room at being awakened at that unheard-of hour. No man could have made more melting appeals for lost souls and back-slidden ministers than did Bounds. Tears ran down his face as he pleaded for us all in that room. I know of no other man on earth to-day, who, if he had followed the same experiment at the same place, in the same room, but would have gone away defeated. But Bounds was all-powerful, all-commanding, all-victorious, when once he knew his cause was just.

After that Convention we took him to our heart and never let him go. God sent him in answer to prayer to settle and establish the writer in the things of God that are foremost and supreme—Prayer, Preaching, and the study of the Bible.

We were constantly with him, in prayer and preaching, for eight precious years. Not a foolish word did we ever hear him utter. He was one of the most intense eagles of God that ever penetrated the spiritual ether. He could not brook delay in rising, or being late for dinner. He would go with me to street meetings often in Brooklyn and listen to the preaching and sing with us those beautiful songs of Wesley and Watts. He often reprimanded me for asking the unconverted to sing of Heaven. Said he: " They have no heart to sing, they do not know God, and God does not hear them. Quit asking sinners to sing the songs of Zion and the Lamb." To what mysterious order of men did Bounds belong, anyway? Have they clean gone out of the world?

Few subjects are better fitted to afford interest in the mind of the fervent Christian reader than the subject Bounds has named: Heaven, A State, A City, A Home. He was so full of the " Heavenly Manna " that God produced through him the spiritual splendour that shines out of every chapter of his wonderful books.

In 1912 I wrote him to come to Brooklyn, N. Y., and spend a while in praying for me and my church. Here are a few extracts from his personal letters to us at this time which show the depths of his thought for a Home in Heaven.

"*Washington, July 1, 1912:* I am thinking more of going to Heaven than to New York. It *is far better*. But it is in God's will. I would enjoy being with you. God seems to have opened the way. I will have to wait on God for New York or Heaven as I am now very feeble. With all love and prayer."

"*December 12 and 13, 1912:* You will pray much. I am turning to you and Chilton. One of you must help me to do the work on my manuscripts that I want finished and published. I could go to you and then you could help me in odd times by prayer and consultation. We would then be together as long as God lets me live for His great work. We can issue the books conjointly and you can keep them if necessary until I die—until God's fitting time to publish." On January 6, 1913, he writes as follows: "Dearly Beloved: A good time praying for you. Be at it early and late. Let your mind live in the spirit of prayer. The thought of *heaven is sweet*. I am right feeble, but will strive to work on and wait for God's time for *heaven*."

He was growing weaker and nearing the other shore when he wrote this letter:

"*April 21, 1913:* God will manage our affairs if we will be filled with His affairs. I am trying to get matters in shape for my manuscripts. I am very feeble. I want to live for God, and then depart and be with Christ. I have an unspeakable desire to know the future, to see it and enjoy it, and to be there—to see and enjoy. God bless you."

The following letters I call dying messages to one whom he loved:

"*Washington, May 10, 1913:* With all love and longing and prayers. God bless and keep you until eternal life. With many trials and tears, I am pressing on. I am still weak, but by sleeping in the day I can get through. When He is ready, I long for the *heavenlies* through Christ."

"*Washington, Ga., May 22, 1913:* Yours came. I have you in prayer, at it early and trying to be at it all the day. God bless you unto eternal life and hasten the day. Go out into the highways and hedges and compel them to come in. Bear your boys on your prayers to the doors *of heaven.* I am getting the *book* ready to send to England. Pray God to open the way for it to His glory. In love and faithful prayer as my strength will allow."

He wrote one card dated June 26, 1913:

"*Washington, Ga.:* In prayful sympathy and love. Hold to the old truth—double distilled."

The above card was the last word to us written by his own hand. On August 9, just before he died, his wife writes: " He was glad to hear from you but soon forgets. My physician says he will never be well again. His last message to you is characteristic: ' Tell him he is on the right line; press it. Have a high standard and hold to it.' "

Then came the telegram announcing his home-going:

" *Washington, Ga., August 24, 1913:* Doctor Bounds went home this afternoon; funeral here to-morrow afternoon.—HATTIE BOUNDS."

His prayer that his manuscripts be left until proper time for publishing has been answered. We have been working and compiling them for the space of six years, off and on, and have good reasons to believe that the Publishers will in due season issue them for the benefit of a world that sorely needs the golden thoughts of such a saint of God as was Edward M. Bounds.

HOMER W. HODGE.

Contents

I

HEAVEN, A PLACE

"If God had told me some time ago that He was about to make me as happy as I could be in this world, and then had told me that He should begin by crippling me in all my limbs, and removing me from all my usual sources of enjoyment, I should have thought it a very strange mode of accomplishing His purpose. And yet, how is His wisdom manifest even in this! for if you should see a man shut up in a close room, idolizing a set of lamps and rejoicing in their light, and you wished to make him truly happy, you would begin by blowing out all his lamps; and then throw open the shutters to let in the light of heaven."

—SAMUEL RUTHERFORD.

HEAVEN is a place. Out of the region of all fancy it is taken and put into the realm of the actual, the local. The revelations of the bare fact that death does not end all, death cannot end all; that man *must* exist to all eternity, that the future may be one of unutterable bliss,—that is the fact. This fact may have many colorings, many symbols, but these are not the main things, nor of the main thing. Heaven does not float around. It is not made of air, thin air. It is real, a country, a clime, a home sacred affinities draw to the spot. Divine assurance settles and fixes the fact.

13

Heaven might be a reality, but simply a state. In its location and grasp it might be airy, volatile. The Bible statement is of a place. One of the main ideas contained in the heavenly symbol, of a city, is place, location, a settled place, in contrast with a pilgrim state, unsettled and temporary.

The strong argument for heaven as a place centers in, and clusters about Jesus. The man Jesus, bearing a man's form, the body He wore on earth, has a place assigned Him—a high place.

" Wherefore God also hath highly exalted him, and given him a name which is above every name: That at the name of Jesus every knee should bow, of things in heaven, and things in earth, and things under the earth; And that every tongue should confess that Jesus Christ is Lord, to the glory of God the Father " (Phil. 2:9-11),

" Whom he raised from the dead and set him at his right hand in the heavenly places, Far above all principality, and power, and might, and dominion, and every name that is named, not only in this world, but also in that which is to come: And hath put all things under his feet, and gave him to be head over all things to the church, which is his body, the fulness of him that filleth all in all " (Ephes. 1:20-23).

This excellence and dignity is all conclusive of a place of high honor, the best, the most royal in the heavenly world.

" God who at sundry times and in divers manners

spake in time past unto the fathers by the prophets, Hath in these last days spoken unto us by his Son, whom he hath appointed heir to all things, by whom also he made the worlds; Who being the brightness of his glory, and the express image of his person, and upholding all things by the word of his power, when he had by himself purged our sins, sat down on the right hand of the Majesty on high " (Heb. 1: 1-3).

These all bespeak His place among the home places of God's many mansioned country. "Who is gone into heaven, and is on the right hand of God; angels and authorities and powers being made subject unto him."

These are figures of Christ's exaltation and location. They are figures of a place. Jesus wants us with Him. To see and share His glory. He dwells in a place. A place which honors and glorifies His person and presence. His business is not to be enthroned and receive honor, but He is there for us, to prepare a place for us.

"Father, I will that they also, whom thou hast given me, be with me where I am; that they may behold my glory, which thou hast given me" (John 17: 24).

Heaven in the Bible is represented as a place in contrast with earth. The earth is a place, but unstable, insecure, fleeting. Heaven is stable, secure, eternal.

"For here have we no continuing city, but we seek one to come" (Heb. 13:14).

How marked the contrast between earth and heaven! Earth is but a pilgrim's stay, a pilgrim's journey, a pilgrim's tent. Heaven is a city, permanent, God-planned, God-built, whose foundations are as stable as God's throne.

"By faith Abraham, when he was called to go out into a place which he should after receive for an inheritance, obeyed; and he went out not knowing whither he went. By faith, he sojourned in the land of promise, as in a strange country, dwelling in tabernacles with Isaac and Jacob, the heirs with him of the same promise: For he looked for a city which hath foundations, whose builder and maker is God" (Heb. 11:8-9).

The Bible reveals heaven as a place. It is measured off, has its appointed metes and bounds, as definite place as a city, a walled city. It has its inside and its outside. Heaven is within the city, hell is without.

"For without are dogs, and sorcerers, and whoremongers, and murderers, and idolaters, and whosoever loveth and maketh a lie" (Rev. 22:15).

Heaven is a *place*. Not airy, impalpable, delocalized, is heaven. "I go," said Jesus, "to prepare a *place* for you." That means locality, something settled. Heaven has its deep, strong colorings, its metes and bounds on God's map.

In God's house, Jesus declares, there are many mansions. The New Version has it in the margin, "abiding places." In God's many homes, one home was to be theirs, a place, a home prepared for them. This was the solace to the disciples, saddened as they were. "Going to prepare a place for them," is the purpose and fact in regard to the going of Christ. Nothing can be simpler, more explicit, more downright honest than this revelation to them of Christ's purpose and plans. As though He had said, "Earth is a place where we have been abiding. We can abide together no longer here, but God has many other abiding places. I go to select one of these places for you; when it is ready I will come and take you there, and we will be together in place as well as in spirit, 'that where I am, there ye may be also.'" "United again," Alford says, commenting on this statement of our Lord. "His taking His people to Himself to be where He is," is begun in His Resurrection, carried on in the spiritual life, the making them ready for the place prepared.

Jesus uses the term, "prepare a place." The term means, make the necessary preparation, get everything ready, a figure drawn from the eastern custom of sending on before kings persons to level the roads and make them passable. Jesus is our pioneer, gone to prepare heaven for us. A place

made ready it will be. Its antitype was Canaan, a
place and a prepared place. Israel did not have to
pioneer the way, build cities, or homes. Homes
and cities were already built for them. They had
to do nothing but simply to enter in, possess and
enjoy. As Canaan was but a feeble type of
heaven, so its preparation was but a faint shadow
of the preparation which will be made for us in
heaven, a city God-built, homes not made with
hands, eternal in the heavens.

As Jesus Christ drew near to the end, in the last
conversation on the eve of His death, important
things, most important, all important things, engaged His attention. He must commit to His disciples the interests of His kingdom. Heaven was
all important. Heaven was to be kept in eye and
heart all the time. He speaks of heaven. Their
deep spiritual life, their personal holiness, their
conscious abiding in Christ, all this was all important. Of this Christ spake in His last words,
sacred words, holy words, of the necessity of
Christ-life and Christ-likeness.

What could be clearer, more hope-giving, more
conclusive than the utterance of Christ on the
verge of His going away! His disciples were sor-
rowfully impressed, deeply touched, and depressed
by the fact of His leaving them. He challenges
their faith in Himself and links Himself inseparably as the object of their faith with God.

Peter views heaven as a place, an inheritance

to be sought for, a possession awaiting us. He is scarcely less enraptured by the glorious vision and reversion, its location and certainty than Paul.

"Blessed be the God and Father of our Lord Jesus Christ, which according to his abundant mercy hath begotten us again unto a lively hope by the resurrection of Jesus Christ from the dead, to an inheritance, incorruptible, and undefiled, and that fadeth not away, reserved in heaven for you, who are kept by the power of God through faith unto salvation ready to be revealed in the last time" (1 Peter 1:3–5).

This is no impalpable state without local habitation, or merely a name. It is located, named definitely, and definitely described.

John had a picture of heaven which located it. The picture is for charm, comfort and for strength.

"After this I beheld, and, lo, a great multitude, which no man could number, of all nations, and kindreds, and people, and tongues, stood before the throne, and before the Lamb, clothed with white robes, and palms in their hands; And cried with a loud voice, saying, Salvation to our God, which sitteth upon the throne, and unto the Lamb. And all the angels stood round about the throne, and about the elders and the four beasts, and fell before the throne on their faces, and worshipped God. Saying, Amen: Blessing, and glory, and wisdom, and thanksgiving, and honor, and power, and might, be

unto our God for ever and ever. Amen. And one
of the elders answered, saying unto me, What are
these which are arrayed in white robes? and whence
came they? And I said unto him, Sir, thou knowest.
And he said to me, These are they which came out
of great tribulation, and have washed their robes, and
made them white in the blood of the Lamb. Therefore are they before the throne of God, and serve
him day and night in his temple: and he that sitteth
on the throne shall dwell among them. They shall
hunger no more, neither thirst any more; neither
shall the sun light upon them, nor any heat. For the
Lamb which is in the midst of the thone shall feed
them, and shall lead them unto living fountains of
waters: and God shall wipe away all tears from their
eyes " (Rev. 7:9–17).

"To-day shalt thou be with me in Paradise,"
was the answer of Jesus to the prayer of the dying
thief. "Through the gates into the city," repre-
sents a place. So also "Absent from the body to
be present with the Lord" indicates locality. Elijah and Enoch are in their bodies.

The future of the saint will not be impalpable
and transitory, but defined, limited, real as soul and
body will be real. The glorified will not be pilgrims, transient visitors, or tenants at wiil, but
settled, permanent, walled, established by title,
through eternity by warrantee deed, signed, sealed,
recorded, possession given. No renters, no lessees
of heaven, but all property and home-owners.

Heaven's patent is issued to guarantee right and title. In fact it is ours before we get there. It is reserved for us, it is guarded for us, our names of ownership are engraven, jeweled on our heavenly home.

Heaven is a *house*, "a house not made with hands eternal in the heavens." In this the apostle is drawing a contrast between a tent, its frailty, its temporary nature and the permanency of heaven. "For we know," says the apostle, "that if our earthly house of this tabernacle were dissolved we have a building of God, an house not made with hands eternal in the heavens."

All earthly houses however beautiful, costly, and enduring they may be, are made with earthly hands and subject to decay. The marks of their death are on them, laid in their very foundations. The houses of heaven are God-built, and are as enduring and incorruptible as their builder. We will have bodies after the resurrection, transfigured they will be after the model of Christ's glorious body. The transfiguration will refine and spiritualize the substance of our bodies, but we will require houses then to locate us as now. What houses they will be! fitted essentially for every use, employment, and enjoyment of the heavenly citizens, worthy of God their builder, reflecting honor on and bringing glory to Him by the untold beauty, magnificence, and grandeur of these God-built houses. Whatever the house as used by Paul in this extract may mean, whether it is used to signify the glorious body which shall be the habitation of our spirits, or whether he has reference to some glorious structure outside of ourselves, fitted for home uses, as our houses are, it is all the same God-built mansion for spirit, or for body and spirit immortalized. It is " a building of God not made with hands eternal in the heavens." It will be for us; we shall be in it. A thing of beauty and joy forever and ever, Amen! ·

Paul again asserts the security and confidence of heaven:

"We are always confident I say, and willing rather to be absent from the body and to be at home with the Lord" (2 Cor. 5:6).

Home is always a place, the heart's place, the place to which longings draw, and around which sweet memories cluster.

Paul was caught up into paradise, into the third heaven. All these passages and others have in them, in intention and spirit, a place. Lazarus was carried by the angels and located in Abraham's bosom.

In the Bible the fact also is taken for granted that heaven is a place, stable, enduring, all attractive, in contrast with the veering nature and transitory conditions of our earth's sojourn. If the description in the Revelation of John be in any wise a description of the material aspects of heaven, the place is one of matchless and exquisite beauty, " incorruptible, undefiled, that fadeth not away."

Stephen the first martyr was a man full of faith and the Holy Spirit. In the presence of a cruel murderous death and an infuriated mob, he had the sight and calm of heaven.

" But he being full of the Holy Ghost, looked up steadfastly into heaven, and saw the glory of God, and Jesus standing on the right hand of God. And said, Behold, I see the heavens opened, and the Son of man standing on the right hand of God. Then they cried out with a loud voice, and stopped their ears, and ran upon him with one accord, And cast him out of the city, and stoned him: and the witnesses laid down their clothes at a young man's feet, whose name was Saul. And they stoned Stephen, calling upon God, and saying, Lord Jesus, receive my spirit. And he kneeled down, and cried with a loud voice, Lord, lay not this sin to their charge. And when he had said this, he fell asleep" (Acts 7: 55-60).

Jesus declares, "I came down from heaven."
He is declared in the sacred scriptures to be " The second man from heaven." Much shall we learn from Him of heaven. From heaven He came, for heaven He suffered. In heaven He lived, to heaven He returned. Born in heaven, living in heaven, breathing the air of heaven, speaking the language of heaven, longing for heaven,

it would be strange if we did not hear from His lips much of heaven.

In familiar language He constantly impresses us with the fact that heaven is a place. What are the words in his memorable conversation with Nicodemus but a contrast of places—earth and heaven and His own identification, and location with the one!

" If I have told you earthly things and ye believe not, how shall ye believe, if I tell you of heavenly things? And no man hath ascended up to heaven, but he that came down from heaven, even the Son of man which is in heaven " (John 3: 12–13).

We are well assured that we shall hear much from His lips of heaven. So He begins His Beatitudes, " Blessed are the poor in spirit for theirs is the kingdom of heaven " (Matt. 5: 3).

This sermon on the mount among His first utterances, if not the very first, begins with heaven. He teaches us to let our light shine that we may glorify our Father in heaven; that except our righteousness exceed the righteousness of the scribes and Pharisees we shall in no case enter into the kingdom of heaven. So He begins His divine mission and marvelous career with heaven accepted, recognized as a matter of course, in full force and to the front. His first preaching was saturated with the idea of the principles of heaven. " Repent," He said, " for the kingdom of heaven is at hand." The first foundation stone of spiritual character is cemented, impregnated with the same. The first utterance of His first sermon is a beatitude of the kingdom of heaven. The diamond of all diamonds of character is, " Blessed are the pure in heart for they shall see God." What includes, seeing, knowing, and loving God, but it includes and finds its full realization in heaven. To see God, to see Him in everything, in every tear that dims the eye or breaks the heart—that is heaven, heaven begun on earth. To see God—that is heaven, the highest heaven, heaven to all eternity. " For now we see through a glass, darkly; but then face to face: now I know in part; but then shall I know even as also I am known " (1 Cor. 13: 12).

He brings us into the presence of the children and their character, and we see the child's inheritance, " if children then heirs." " Blessed are the peacemakers; for they shall be called the children of God " (Matt. 5: 9).

The next Beatitude reads, " Blessed are they which are persecuted for righteousness' sake: for theirs is the kingdom of heaven." This leads the way to the last: " Blessed are they which are persecuted for righteousness' sake: for theirs is the kingdom of heaven." " Blessed are ye, when men shall revile you, and persecute you, and shall say all manner of evil against you falsely, for my sake. Rejoice, and be exceeding glad: for great is your reward in heaven, for so persecuted they

the prophets which were before you" (Matt.
5: 10–12).

Jesus at the very beginning and in His first call
to discipleship stimulates and connects that call
with all the alluring weight, comfort, and hope of
heaven. Heaven is at the foundation of the system of Jesus, its first thought, brightest hope,
strongest faith. Their Father, He tells them, is in
heaven, a place worthy the abode of God, and they
must so demean themselves as to reflect glory on
their Father in heaven. The righteousness of
His followers must exceed the righteousness of the
Scribes and Pharisees, else the glories of heaven
would never be theirs. The commonplace, gener-
ally current piety will not bring heaven. Heaven in
the teaching of Jesus is God's throne. Earth His
footstool. As the throne excels in honor, character, material, and uses the footstool, so does
heaven excel earth. How much, who can tell?
He will not let it get out of their mind that their
Father is in heaven, a place, defined, located, and
that they are His children; they must be like Him
to share His character, imitate His conduct, to
share His heaven. He keeps before us constantly
that heaven is His home. The Father's character
must be the children's character, the Father's conduct, the children's conduct, the Father's place, the
children's place, the Father's home, the children's
home.

"Ye have heard that it hath been said, Thou shalt

love thy neighbor, and hate thine enemy. But I say unto you, Love your enemies, bless them that curse you, do good to them that hate you, and pray for them which despitefully use you, and persecute you; That ye may be the children of your Father which is in heaven, for he maketh his sun to rise on the evil and the good, and sendeth his rain on the just and on the unjust. For if ye love them which love you, what reward have ye? do not even the publicans the same? And if ye salute your brethren only, what do ye more than others? do not even the publicans so? Be ye therefore perfect, even as your Father which is in heaven is perfect " (Matt. 5 : 43–48).

He faces and prefaces duties with heaven as the home of our Father. Almsgiving, prayer and fasting take their coloring, and their obligation from " Our Father who art in heaven." Heaven is His dwelling place, and the very place itself receives its glory from the Father. The Father's name and the Father's dwelling place are to be hallowed. Heaven is not only the home of God, but it is to be the pattern after which earth is to be fashioned. Earth ought to look to heaven, its harmony, its beauty, its ecstasy, all due to implicit obedience to God's will, and learn how to rival heaven. But instead earth is devoted to its own fashions, and is even ready to forget the higher and holier place after which it should type.

Jesus keeps the place, the being, the order, and

beauty of heaven, ever before us and hangs them
all around the Father's house, the trappings and
decorations of His abode, saying, be like God. He
is your Father. Children be like your Father.
Heaven is His home. Make your home like His.

Earth is unsafe, says Jesus. Thieves are here,
treasures are lost here. Moths are here. Finest
silks and costliest robes are eaten. Rust is here.
Richest jewels and finest gold, costliest metals cor-
rode and rust. Heaven is a place, as really as earth
is a place, a place of absolute safety. Thieves are
never there. No robberies ever occur on its plains
or in its cities. Moths are not known there. Its
spotless robes have never been defiled by their
touch. Its precious stones and metals know not
the corroding touch of rust. All is pure, polished,
glittering and forever secure. How emphatic and
absolute the command for safety and obedience!

"Lay not up for yourselves treasures upon earth,
where moth and rust doth corrupt, and where thieves
break through and steal: But lay up for yourselves
treasures in heaven, where neither moth nor rust doth
corrupt, and where thieves do not break through nor
steal: For where your treasure is, there will your
heart be also. The light of the body is the eye: if
therefore thine eye be single, thy whole body shall
be full of light. But if thine eye be evil, thy whole
body shall be full of darkness. If therefore the light
that is in thee be darkness, how great is that darkness!" (Matt. 6: 20–23).

How the divine teacher emphasizes heaven! He wants our hearts to be there. They must be there, if we ever get there. The heart is the soul, the being, the man. Safety is in heaven. Put your values there only, put your heart there. No tears are there to flood your heart, no sorrows there to break it, no losses there to grieve and embitter. Put your heart in heaven, says Jesus, that it may be sweet, and whole, and joyful. Put your treasures in heaven, says Jesus, and all will be light and clear, cloudless and strong. Don't divide between heaven and earth. If so, the light will be mixed, confused and confusing, and turn the darkness into darkness, all the darker for the light lost in it. Don't divide between heaven and earth, says Jesus.

"No man can serve two masters, for either he will hate the one and love the other; or else he will hold to the one and despise the other. Ye cannot serve God and mammon."

Anxiety about food and raiment, the fears hidden in the womb of to-morrow, have mastered many a soul, breeded fears and disrooted faith. Jesus Christ shows that the cause of these anxieties and carefulness results from lack of faith in our Father in heaven, and as their only infallible cure, He puts on an absorbing pursuit of heaven; "Seek ye first the kingdom of God and his righteousness, and all these things shall be added to you." He would quiet our anxieties by stressing the fact that our "Heavenly Father knoweth that ye have need of all these things," by linking us constantly with our Father, His ability and solicitude for us. With heaven His abode and ours, Jesus would calm our hearts, and set them on heaven and its pursuits, which is impossible when earthly need and necessaries bewilder and engross. Heaven to Jesus is the real place. The Father's place and home.

> Let others seek a home below,
> Which flames devour, or waves o'erflow,
> Be mine a happier lot, to own
> A heavenly mansion near the throne.
>
> Then fail this earth, let stars decline,
> And sun and moon refuse to shine,
> All nature sink and cease to be,
> That heavenly mansion stands for me.
>   —*William Hunter.*

II

HEAVEN, A CITY

"If contentment were here, heaven were not heaven. I wonder that ever a child of God should have a sad heart, considering what his Lord is preparing for him. I know not a thing worth the buying but heaven."

—SAMUEL RUTHERFORD.

THE city is of heavenly and divine birth, shaped and built by God in heavenly mold with heavenly air about her. The heavenly life will come from God directly, and will be heavenly, not earthly. Many earthly things, by chance, by happenings and of direct purpose and appointment, shape our earthly lives, but in a direct and most evident and all inclusive way, our heavenly lives will be from God, and the air and conditions of heaven will shape them. Earth will not be forgotten, but the former things will scarcely be remembered. Nor will the things of old be considered, but crowded out, overwhelmed and retired by the magnificent grandeur, ever new and expanding glories of the present. Earth will be too little, its most sacred relations, its most pleasing things all too poor to come into mind in heaven.

"And I, John, saw the holy city, new Jerusalem, coming down from God out of heaven, prepared as a bride adorned for her husband. And I heard a great voice out of heaven saying, Behold, the tabernacle of God is with men, and he will dwell with them, and they shall be his people, and God himself shall be with them, and be their God. And God shall wipe away all tears from their eyes; and there shall be no more death, neither sorrow, nor crying, neither shall there be any more pain: for the former things are passed away. And he that sat upon the throne said, Behold, I make all things new" (Rev. 21: 1-5).

A transfigured mind and memory, a purified thought and love, a transfigured body, shining like a sun in noonday splendor, which has no eclipse and fears no night—a transfigured heaven and earth—this will be the saint's eternal inheritance.

God's power and glory making all things new— a bride adorned for her husband—the marriage hour—the bridal array—one and all are emblems of the beauty of the heavenly life. The marriage of heaven and earth on their festal day. Heaven the place of perfect beauty, perfect taste, perfect joy—the bridal life and all that life—this be heaven's honeymoon.

The tabernacle has reference to the place where God dwells and manifested Himself to Moses. God will be essentially and immediately present with man in the heavenly world. God shall be with them in a sense in which He is not with them in this life. They will draw their being and their blessing directly from Him without the aid of intermediaries. "And I saw no temple therein: for the Lord God almighty and the Lamb are the temple of it. And the city had no need of the sun, neither of the moon, to shine in it: for the glory of God did lighten it, and the Lamb is the light thereof."

And again it is said: "And they need no candle, neither light of the sun; for the Lord God giveth them light." In this life we cannot understand this. Secondary causes are the agencies through which God ministers to us in this world. In that higher life these agencies will not intervene and hide God, but with open vision, face to face, we shall see Him. No temple there, no gorgeous temple service, no brilliant sun to shine, no simpler service will be there. The glory of God, brighter than the light of a thousand suns, will be our light, and the mild sweet rays from the Lamb will cast their radiance over all the land, dispelling darkness and gloom and sorrow. "For there shall be no night there," and to make it strong and clear it is declared, the second time, "And there shall be no night there."

In heaven no tears will be shed, for God will wipe all tears from their eyes. "There shall be no death, neither sorrow nor crying nor pain." What a changed world! How difficult to imagine such

a world! Tears are the sad heritage of this life.
Sorrow and pain flow from a thousand sources,
and deepen and widen and darken earth's sorrow.
Our sweetest relations give birth to our greatest
sorrows. Our distresses often flow from our joys.
Death reigns. All this will be changed, and everything which gives pain and sorrow anyway, will be
forever barred from heaven. God will shut it out.
How bright the eyes undimmed by a tear! How
strong and free our souls and bodies will be, utter
and eternal strangers to pain! How bright and
joyous our hearts, with never a cloud, never a sorrow. How full of richest and largest life, un-
touched by decay, unshadowed by death, will
heaven be!

All things are to be made new. No marks of
age, no common things, no freshened or repainted
old things, but absolutely new, all things will be—
a new world, a new life, a new career, a new history, new environments, new conditions, new employments, new destiny, *all, all* things will be new.
World dreams, pictures, poetry, fiction, music—
all have failed to give the faintest idea of that new
world and its marvelous life, its melody, and
charms. To live there is a rapture, ecstasy, ineffable, and full of glory. Its climax is, " He that
overcometh shall inherit all things; and I will be
his God, and he shall be my son." It is the wonder
and spectacle of angels.

Type and shadow, precept and promise, both in

the Old and New Testaments are given tokens and seals of the saints' inheritance after death. No truth is fuller in statement, more necessary to man, none more in accordance with God's character, none more necessary to His glory, than the truth, and doctrine of heaven. An eternal heaven of unsullied purity, of unalloyed bliss through its endless years, is a doctrine which enables man and honors God. The existence of heaven and its matchless perfection is a truth, based upon the advent, the person and work of Jesus Christ, for He makes heaven. Christ is the way to heaven.

Many are the lessons in the Bible, which declare in word, by figure and by picture the fact of heaven. Heaven lies beyond this life. It is located in another world. The boundary line, death, must be crossed ere its portals can be entered, its happy land possessed and enjoyed.

Among the many varied illustrations by which the fact and nature of heaven are conveyed to us, that of a city is conspicuous. It seems to convey more clearly and fully the idea and characteristic of that unseen and to us unknown land. A city teems with life. A busy life-stirred and life-stirring scene is a city, life in its most opulent and strenuous form. Heaven is a city of life. It has never felt the touch, or chill of death. A life unlimited by conditions, or time, unrestrained by any of the environments of this earthly life. Graves have never been digged there, cemeteries are unknown, tombstones and coffins are alien to that land. A city of life heaven is, majestic, glorious life—a life which knows no tears, never felt a sorrow—eternal, fadeless, decayless life.

A city is a picture of closest union. Life there is forced into closest proximity. Unity, compactness, nearness, are the essentials to the city life.

Heaven is the place of unity, nearness. Earth is broken into discord. Separation is the law of earth. There are no distances in heaven. Oceans and mountains are not. It is called the " Beloved City." Affections center there, longings go thither in strong restless current. Beloved of earth and beloved of heaven, the saintly of earth have turned their feet to heaven and placed their heart's dearest love there. Angels hold it in tenderest love. Friends are there. In that city they have found their home. Centuries have come and gone since the tired feet of earth's saintly pilgrims found sweet rest and home in that beloved city. None ever go out of that city. Love holds them. " The city of my God," says Christ, " the city of the Living God. God hath prepared for them a city, a city that hath foundations, whose maker and builder is God." God has much to do, everything to do with that city. He drew its plans, digged and laid its deep foundations. God built it, God fitted it, God finished it. God lives in it. All life is there, all life direct from God, life in its fulness, vigor, brightness. God is its life. Its maker and builder is God.

God is its Architect and Contractor; no archangel's matchless taste and incomparable genius were used in drafting the plan of this glorious city, this eternal inheritance. God drew the plan. The exhaustless stores of God's own wisdom, His divine skill and faultless taste brought into perfect perfection the design of that City which was to be the abiding home of His children. Neither were the ability and resources of an archangel brought into requisition to execute the high and holy design. God was its builder. He only could carry out the original. The God who laid the deep foundations of the world, and brought into being and order its mightily framed and mighty movements, condescends to enter again into the work of creation, and builds a city as the superb home for His elect ones of earth.

No night with its darkness rests as a pall on this heavenly city. It is emphatically called, "the city of the living God." God is more immediately, more personally, more gloriously there than elsewhere. Life is there with God as its immediate source and supply, and it is life in its most opulent fulness, and redolent of all that is sweet, gracious, and attractive, and free from all that could in any way affect the perfection of its joy, or restrain or stint its endless advance. Glorious city—God-built, glorious inhabitants—who can paint its glories!

Who can picture the glories of its blissful inhabitants? It would be a little heaven to see the city and get a sight of its ravished and princely citizens.

It is a walled city, for protection, and jeweled are its walls. A city was a treasure deposit. Its walls its security. The treasure safe. The New Jerusalem it is called not only in opposition to and distinction from the Old Jerusalem, but also to designate its freshness, forever new. Never is it to know decay or dulness. It is called the heavenly Jerusalem to distinguish it from the earthly one, and also to emphasize its glories. The earthly Jerusalem was the center of Jewish hopes. Their hearts were there. No song, nothing but sadness and exile, when away from it. Their hearts were always trembling to that pole, their prayers were made with windows open to Jerusalem. All this but symbolizes what the heavenly Jerusalem should be to us. "If I forget thee, O Jerusalem, let my right hand forget her cunning. If I do not remember thee, let my tongue cleave to the roof of my mouth; if I prefer not Jerusalem above my chief joy." Heaven ought to be far more to us than Jerusalem was to the Jew. In this "we groan earnestly desiring to be clothed upon with our house which is from heaven."

These Bible symbols are designed to draw, stir and allure, and also to instruct us in the nature of heaven so far as earth by language can convey eternal and heavenly things. What is heaven, by the Bible is called a city. This is a familiar Bible symbol of heaven—a city, a great city, a city that hath foundations, the city of the living God. It is not by accident that this term is a familiarized and favorite one. It is suggestive of heaven's manifold nature.

Out of deference to Jewish sanctities and devotion and as a memorial, it was called " The New Jerusalem." The Jew will find full compensation for the loss of his earthly Jerusalem in this new city which will endure eternally without decay of luster, renown or glory.

The term "city" is a familiar type of the heavenly land and of the heavenly life, a city being the center of power and of life. A great city is heaven. All the principles and facts, of which the term city is the exponent, find their full expression there. A jeweled and a golden city express the unsurpassed loveliness and preciousness of that country and its life. The jewels are in the foundations of its walls and gold is the substance of which its pavements are made. The most costly materials of earth are used for the lowest and most common uses of heaven, and if its most common and meanest things are jeweled and golden, we have no figures or values to represent the exceeding richness of its higher things. A Great City it is, God's capital, effulgent with all the glory of His presence.

Heaven is called a city, in reference to the original meaning of the word city, " fulness, throng."

Heaven will be full. "An innumerable company which no man can number" will gather within its walls. Not sparsely settled will heaven be. Its thoroughfares will be crowded, its golden pavements will be pressed by throngs of enraptured feet.

The road to heaven is indeed narrow, the gate straight, and few there be that find it, but each community, each generation contributes its few, who dare to be singular, who are brave enough to walk and struggle alone, but on through the revolving ages, the few precious ones are being housed in heaven until the aggregate will be great. If you and I miss that happy land, others will shoulder the cross, pass out of the popular, pleasing wide way, and make the solitary journey, and take our crown which we have so ignobly and foolishly lost.

A city is the symbol of life in its magnificence, perfections and glory. Heaven will be the realization of all this. Doubtless in this figure of a city is found the closeness of sympathy, love, and fellowship which will abound there.

It is called by Scripture designation and contrast, "a *continuing* city." The inconstant, ephemeral nature of earth's most substantial and social things is proverbial. Poetry and fiction speak of it. It is part of the sad experience of life, and the most cursory observation confirms experience, that earth is mutable, its fairest flowers fade away, and its most precious joys soon wither. But heaven is enduring. It is not the pilgrim's inn. It is home, it abides, settled forever.

A "prepared city," ready, fitted up, complete. No virgin soil, nor virgin forests will salute us. There no toil in building homes, no taxing labor to build, arrange, culture will face us; but everything ready, everything anticipated, furnished, by a taste and care, a knowledge and ability which knows all wants, furnishes all comforts, supplies all luxuries, which stops not at expense.

A "holy city" pure, unsullied in character, nothing which stains, nothing impure can gain an entrance there. Everything is as brilliant as the diamond and as pure. It is said to be great in its goodness and light, great in its attractive power, and great in frame, in beauty and in grandeur. All about the city is most exquisite in charms, most precious in value, most costly in richness.

That it is a holy city is more to our purpose and for our good than its greatness. The term " holy " —its origin baffles the critics to define with certainty and clearness. It certainly means separated to God, devoted to Him. It certainly means purity. Earthly cities are great, but their purity is not infrequently in the inverse ratio to their greatness. In heaven greatness is never divorced from goodness. Not so on earth. Heaven is a city whose purity clarifies its atmosphere and causes it to sparkle and glitter like crystal. A city whose light is in its purity, its brightness and permanency, an emanation from God and the Lamb.

"And there came unto me one of the seven angels which had the seven vials full of the seven last plagues, and talked with me saying, Come hither, I will shew thee the bride, the Lamb's wife. And he carried me away in the spirit to a great and high mountain, and shewed me that great city, the holy Jerusalem, descending out of heaven from God. Having the glory of God: and her light was like unto a stone most precious, even like a jasper stone, clear as crystal; And had a wall great and high " (Rev. 21:9–12).

It took the light and power of the Spirit and the perspective elevation and sublimity of a mountain top to view this city in its exhaustless magnificence and the dazzling charms of its ever increasing glory. What grandeur in that vision, the ecstasy of the spirit, the entrancing city, and the inspiration, awe, sublimity of the great and high mountains! All these heightened and made the view ravishing, but could transfer but a faint resemblance to the reality. It is a picture of exquisite and fadeless beauty, but a picture only. The life, the reality, the substance, no inspired trance, no grand and lofty mountain view could portray.

She had " the glory of God "—what is that? Who can tell? God was there, as we have been told, but " the glory of God," the brightest, the highest, and the greatest display and revelations of

God, the most effulgent brightness of His uncreated glory. It is certainly the highest order of brightness, the completed exhibition of highest excellence, the supreme beauty. All comprehensive of all glory is the expression, " the glory of God," not simply God, but the preëminent and conspicuous manifestation of all that is glorious, majestic, all glorious in God. The revelation of God is this glory, and it forms the light, blessedness and splendor of the city. What a land! What a life! where the glory of God constitutes the loveliness and glory of the land. The opulence and wealth of its life! Her light was like a stone most precious. God's glory the sun! The light coming from such a sun would dazzle and flame like earth's most costly, beautiful, effulgent, and sparkling diamond.

The walls and the gates find their expressive significance in Isaiah: " Thy walls are salvation and thy gates praise." Behold I will lay thy stones with fair colors and lay thy foundations with sapphires, and will make the windows of agates and thy gates of carbuncles and all thy borders of pleasant stones. We have a strong city: " Salvation will God appoint for walls and bulwarks."

The walls represent the strength and power of the salvation of the heavenly life. So evident and mighty are the forces of their salvation in heaven that it fills with transporting rapture and goes out with unrestrained, spontaneous and mighty energy:

"After this I beheld and, lo, a great multitude, which no man could number, of all nations, and kindreds, and people, and tongues, stood before the throne, and before the Lamb, clothed with white robes, and palms in their hands: And cried with a loud voice, saying, Salvation to our God which sitteth upon the throne, and unto the Lamb. And all the angels stood round about the throne, and about the elders and the four living creatures, and fell before the throne on their faces, and worshipped God, saying, Amen: Blessing, and glory, and wisdom, and thanksgiving, and honor, and power, and might, be unto our God for ever and ever. Amen" (Rev. 7:9–12).

Salvation ought to be much to us on earth, in present joy, unspeakable and full of glory, and its most inspiring hope. But much as it is to us, it is much more to them in heaven. We have the rill, they its ocean streams; we have the glitter and mildness of its starlight, they have the sun in his unclouded strength.

The wall is great and high:

"And the wall of the city had twelve foundations, and in them the names of the twelve apostles of the Lamb. . . . And the building of the wall of it was of jasper: and the city was pure gold, like unto clear glass. And the foundations of the wall of the city were garnished with all manner of precious stones" (Rev. 21:14–19).

The walls are for protection, the foundations of

which are twelve, which indicates their strength, while the jewels represent the beauty and precious- ness of its strength. The heavenly life will be a protected life, walled in by massive strength and jeweled beauty, to adorn and enrich. We will be held in heaven. We will go out no more. The motives and influences which hold us to heaven will be strong, but not iron, dull, heavy and strong. Jasper are the walls and all the twelve foundations are gemmed with every variety of precious stones. The forces binding us to heaven will not imprison us, but will hold us there by forces as strong as walls of iron, and as resplendent as jasper—as strong as twelve foundations can make it, but as rich, as various, as brightly glorious, as the bril- liants which emblazon each.

The building material of the walls of the city was jasper. We have in the third chapter this description of God: "And immediately I was in the Spirit: and, behold, a throne was set in heaven, and one sat on the throne. And he that sat was to look upon like a jasper and a sardine stone."

How remarkable are the walls of the heavenly city, made out of the same material! How closely God and His city are allied and unified, when this same book says:

" Him that overcometh will I make a pillar in the temple of my God, and he shall go no more out: and I will write upon him the name of my God, and the name of the city of my God, which is new Jerusalem, which cometh down out of heaven, from my God: and I will write upon him my new name" (Rev. 3: 12).

The city was pure gold, transparent, and reflecting every form of beauty, far surpassing in richness and purity and value any earthly gold.

Its walls are made of jasper—foundations of jewels of every hue and value,—gates of pearl— city, pure transparent gold. All figures and values and beauty are exhausted in description. What can exceed these! No earthly values of wealth and loveliness! Earthly and angelic vocabularies are exhausted, and yet but the outside is described. What there is of wealth and good inside defies all language to convey, all beauty to describe. Diamonds and gold, all jewels, are valueless and mean and dull compared to that glorious city heaven, its life and its purified beings, the employments and engagements inside those gates of pearl, those walls of jasper.

All these outward adornments, so unparalleled in their value and preciousness, are indicative in their richness and rareness of the principal joys and pursuits of the heavenly life. How godlike are the persons whose stable and precious characters are represented by twelve jeweled foundations! What a glorious land whose light and purity glitter like brilliant diamonds, whose society is as flawless and pure as transparent gold.

" Thy gates praise "—the gates were places of

council, wisdom, adornment and power. The gates were of one pearl each. There are twelve of them, of unrivaled beauty, cost and purity. They are for entrances, and impress us with the unity, purity, and worth of all who enter there. "Those holy gates forever bar pollution, sin and shame." The angels have much to do with the entrance into the heavenly gates, and much to do with the stay in there. All that is termed kingly, all that belongs to honor and glory, are in that heavenly city.

The very pavement, trodden under foot, lowly, and dishonored, is made of earth's purest gold, which mirror the forms of heavenly saints who walk along its streets. The forms are too beautiful to rest their shadows on any substance less precious than gold, and that gold refined and polished to its highest perfection, and those forms too peerless in beauty, not to be reflected and constantly mirrored as they pass along. These forms and images of perfect beauty add much to the charms of the city.

In this world death reigns. There life reigns:

"And he shewed me a pure river of water of life, clear as crystal, proceeding out of the throne of God and of the Lamb. In the midst of the street of it and on either side of the river was there the tree of life which bore twelve manner of fruit, and yielded her fruit every month: and the leaves of the tree shall be for the healing of the nations. And there shall be no more curse, but the throne of God and the

Lamb shall be in it; and his servants shall serve him" (Rev. 22: 1-3).

It will be life in its full vigor, like a river, deep and exhaustless and wide. A river it will be, not a branch, nor well, but a river ever expanding, ever moving on. It is a river of water. All things in heaven will be to refresh and gladden and to give and increase life. A powerful river, it flows out of the throne of God. God's throne is the symbol of God's rule and God's power. Heaven will be the place where God's power shall be seen and felt. He will rule with unlimited power and absolute authority, but the issuance will be the " river of the water of life, clear as crystal." We are constantly reminded that heaven is all purity. Its life is a river, full charged and strong in current, but transparent, mirroring, crystalline in its purity.

The throne is not separate from the Lamb. The Son of God and His atoning sacrifice unite with the throne to make the full deep current of the heavenly life. In the heavenly world, through all its happy life, with every one of its teeming inhabitants, as the source of its most entrancing vision, as the school of its profoundest lessons, it will always and everywhere and in everything be "a Lamb as it had been slain." Forever will the melody of heaven go on:

"And they sung a new song, saying, Thou art

worthy to take the book, and to open the seals
thereof: for thou wast slain, and hast redeemed us to
God by thy blood out of every kindred, and tongue,
and people, and nation; And hast made us unto our
God kings and priests, and we shall reign on the
earth. And I beheld, and I heard the voice of many
angels round about the throne, and the beasts, and
the elders: and the number of them was ten thousand
times ten thousand, and thousands of thousands;
Saying with a loud voice, Worthy is the Lamb that
was slain to receive power, and riches, and wisdom,
and strength, and honour, and glory, and blessing"
(Rev. 5:9–12).

"The Lamb slain from the foundation of the
world." Every new avenue of delight, every new
discovery in the heavenly life, will be the unfolding
of the wonderful mystery, illimitable glories, and
exhaustless power of the Lamb, the Christ crucified, as well as the enthroned God. Everything in
heaven will conspire to further the vigor, expansion, and glory of that life. The tree of life ever
giving out its fruit, with the freshness, frequency,
and energy of monthly crops, and the very leaves,
are health-giving and invigorating. The curse
with its withering and deadening blight! All the
dire effects of Adam's fall shall be removed. No
traces of the first man's blasting steps shall be seen
or felt. The cause of earth's groaning and sighing
shall be destroyed.

Not the power of Adam, nor the dire effects of

sin inherited or committed, but the power of God,
with all its benign and recreating energy and the
power of the cross to redeem, renew and perfect,
will be there.

Service of the highest, most adoring and enrap-
turing form will characterize heaven. All will be
melody and praise, with not a discordant note in its
melody.

Of God, the inhabitants of heaven will have perfect vision. That vision will be the melody, the
study, and the pursuit of glorified spirits. To
know God, and to know more and more of Him,
will be the employment and bliss of heaven. They
will be sealed for Him with His name in their foreheads, the seat of intelligence. The sign of ownership, the distinctive mark of loyalty and consecra-
tion to God, without the hands of church or priest,
of sacrament or ceremony, rite or ritual, is placed
on them, and they come in person to His person,
and from Him they receive directly all His outlay
of treasure each passing moment of the eternal life.
All lesser lights are obscured, all intermediaries retired. God and Christ, with all the fulness of
their Divine and eternal affluence, are in constant,
personal contact and outgoing. The light of God's
presence hides and disperses all the feeble lights of
earth. God shines with ineffable splendor on the
glorified ones, and all the Divine potencies of the
cross lift them to royal privileges. They are not
only priests, but kings to God. Earth has no insight into the exalted glories into which its in-

habitants shall be lifted in heaven, no conception of the grandeur to which they shall be exalted: no thought or imagination of the scepter which will be put into the hands of the heirs when their inheritance is received.

Does the vision of St. John transport and ravish us? Then heaven is the place where our thirstings for Him are satisfied and our vision of Him is perfect, glorious and ineffable.

With what sublime and soothing verity does the Bible declare everywhere the ineffable superiority of the heavenly life, the heavenly home to this earthly life, and to this earthly home. Heaven robes the saints and transports them with a deathless, painless life. Its length is eternal, its conditions are absolute, and there is eternal freedom from every form of evil—and the presence of every form of good and greatness. How glorious is this when its truth possesses us and lifts us above the earthly life with its incomparable littleness and its unmeasurable ills! The heavenly home—a crown of glory—a joy unspeakable and full of glory!

"And there shall be no more curse; but the throne of God and of the Lamb shall be in it; and his servants shall serve him: And they shall see his face; and his name shall be in their foreheads. And there shall be no night there; and they need no candle, neither light of the sun; for the Lord God giveth them light: and they shall reign for ever and ever" (Rev. 22: 3-5).

We are somewhat aware of the difficulties of interpretation when applied to the Revelation of John. The diversities and antagonism of construction are almost endless. But to whatever school of interpretation the truth may attach, one thing is sure that the description of the heavenly Jerusalem in its last chapters, if it be not primarily the description of heaven, it is a pattern of the heavenly, after which the earthly is to be shaped. As Moses' tabernacle was the pattern of the heavenly, so the literal, real heaven, the heaven of fact, and place, the third heaven where God abides and is seen in His unveiled glory, is photographed by John and presented as the model and final results of God's work on earth. The tabernacle was only showed to Moses in the mount, but the pattern of it was shaped by the original in heaven, and the Jew who studied and followed the pattern understood the principles and substance of the original. We study this picture of the heavenly to know what heaven is.

> To that Jerusalem above
>   With singing I repair;
> While in the flesh, my hope and love,
>   My heart and soul, are there:
> There my exalted Saviour stands,
>   My merciful High Priest,
> And still extends his wounded hands,
>   To take me to his breast.
>   —*Charles Wesley.*

III

HEAVEN: A KINGDOM, A CROWN, AN INHERITANCE

"Happy will I be and forever happy, if after death I might hear the melody of those hymns and hallelujahs which the citizens of that celestial kingdom and the squadron of those blessed spirits sing in praise of the eternal king. This is that sweet music which St. John heard in the Revelation, when the inhabitants of heaven sang, 'Let all the world bless thee, O Lord.' To Thee be given all honor and dominion for a world of worlds.—Amen."

—JEREMY TAYLOR.

WHAT magnificence and splendor are there in a kingdom! What ambitions by the desire of possessing a kingdom! What a stimulant this to noblest effort! Heaven is to be won as a kingdom is won. Heaven is to be struggled for as a kingdom is struggled for. Heaven is to stimulate as a kingdom stimulates. The work of grace in the human heart is called a kingdom, the kingdom of grace. Heaven is called a kingdom, the kingdom of glory. "Come ye blessed of my Father, inherit the kingdom prepared for you"—these are the words as Jesus rewards the honored ones who are on His right hand in the day of judgment:

" That ye would walk worthy of God, who hath called you unto his kingdom and glory," warns Paul. Here we have a combination of the two, kingdom and glory. Magnificent combination! " Rich in faith and heirs of the kingdom," says James. " Have an entrance administered abundantly into the everlasting kingdom of our Lord and Saviour Jesus Christ," declares Peter.

The future life is declared to be a throne:

" To him that overcometh, will I grant to sit with me in my throne, even as I also overcame, and am set down with my Father in his throne " (Rev. 3: 21).

A crown it is: " Hold fast that thou hast, that no man take thy crown." It is an incorruptible crown, a crown whose glory never dims, whose power never abates. Paul is speaking of the Isthmian games and its runners, their strenuous self-denial and arduous efforts. " Now they do it to obtain a corruptible crown; but we an incorruptible."

Paul declares at the very point of death: " Henceforth there is laid up for me a crown of righteousness, which the Lord, the righteous judge, shall give me at that day; and not to me only, but unto all them also that love his appearing." "A crown of righteousness," awarded according to rigid demands of inflexible rectitude. "A crown of life!" " Blessed," says James, " is the man that endureth temptation; for when he is tried, he shall receive the crown of life, which the Lord hath promised to them that love him."

Peter declares, "And when the chief Shepherd shall appear, ye shall receive a crown of glory that fadeth not away." How it stimulates to the strictest temperance and self-denial!

" Know ye not that they which run in a race run all, but one receiveth the prize? So run, that ye may obtain. And every man that striveth for the mastery is temperate in all things. Now they do it to obtain a corruptible crown; but we an incorruptible. I therefore so run, not as uncertainly; so fight I, not as one that beateth the air. But I keep under my body and bring it into subjection; lest that by any means, when I have preached to others, I myself should be a castaway " (1 Cor. 9: 24–27).

This was the effect of this incorruptible crown on the chief of the apostles.

How grand and imposing the awards of eternity are! Glory, all preëminence, and effulgence: A kingdom, authority, elevation and grandeur are in it! A throne, that has in it royal dignity, elevation, rule! A crown belongs to kingly heads, to conquerors, and heroes. Kingship belongs to it. Overcomers, conquerors, are they all who enter the realms of life. How greatly were Grecian athletes stimulated by the crown though perishable! But to win these perishable crowns, there were no toils they would not endure, no efforts they could not put forth. The gathered crowds, the spectators of their contest and carriage, the judge and the crown, at the end of the race—all these matchless excitants are presented as ensamples for us in our contest for heaven.

In Revelation we have a sweeping declaration of heirship: " For he that overcometh shall inherit all things; and I will be his God, and he shall be my son " (Chap. 21: 7).

In Colossians we have a combination of reward and inheritance: " Knowing that of the Lord ye shall receive the reward of the inheritance; for ye serve the Lord Christ."

Heaven is called an inheritance. It comes by relationship and heirship:

" For ye have not received the spirit of bondage again to fear; but ye have received the spirit of adoption, whereby we cry, Abba, Father. The spirit himself beareth witness with our spirit, that we are the children of God. And if children, then heirs; heirs of God, and joint heirs with Christ; if so be that we suffer with him, that we may be also glorified together " (Rom. 8: 15-17). And in Galatians (Chap. 4: 6-7) we read: "And because ye are sons, God hath sent forth the spirit of the Son into your hearts, crying, Abba, Father. Wherefore thou art no more a servant, but a son; and if a son, then an heir of God through Christ."

Peter has a magnificent statement of the heirship and the future inheritance of the saints in heaven:

" Blessed be the God and Father of our Lord Jesus Christ, which, according to his abundant mercy, hath begotten us again unto a lively hope by the resurrection of Jesus Christ from the dead, to an inheritance, incorruptible, undefiled, and that fadeth not away, reserved in heaven for you who are kept by the power of God through faith unto salvation" (1 Peter 1:3-5).

It is represented as a gift: " The gift of God is eternal life."

This diversity and wealth of expression as to the character of heaven, and how it comes to us, is seen as a great " reward "; a magnificent and imperishable " inheritance " of fadeless beauty and unending richness; a " prize," the greatest of time or eternity; a " gift," unspeakable and indescribable in all its elements.   The refined and refining stimulant of heaven has produced the saintliest saints, the most heroic heroes, the greatest conquerors, the most self-denying toilers.

How strong are the stimulating forces that heaven awakens!   We could not dispense with them, that is, when held in our mind and hearts as they ought to be held, in deepest conviction, in most ardent faith, and interested loyalty.   These heavenly forces are always strengthening our weakness, elevating our depression, brightening our darkness—always calling us to purity and nobleness, always charging us to awaken to righteousness and sin not.   The mighty quickener of faith is heaven. The only sure and solid foundation of hope is heaven. The only solution of earth's mysteries, the only righter of earth's wrongs, the only divorce from earth to heaven, the only cure for worldliness, is heaven. We need such an infusion of heaven into our faith and hope as will create a homesickness for that blessed place. God's home place is heaven. Eternal life and all good were born there and flourish there. All life, all happiness, all beauty, all glory, are native to the home of God.

And all this belongs to and awaits the heirs of God in heaven. What a glorious inheritance! What a pleasing prospect!

'Tis God's all-animating voice
    That calls thee from on high;
'Tis his own hand presents the prize
    To thine aspiring eye—

That prize, with peerless glories bright,
    Which shall new luster boast,
When victors' wreaths and monarchs' gems
    Shall blend in common dust.

Blest Saviour, introduced by thee,
    Have I my race begun;
And, crowned with victory, at thy feet
    I'll lay my honors down.
                    —*Philip Doddridge.*

IV

PARADISE AND ETERNAL LIFE

"Go on, and faint not. Something of yours is in heaven, beside the flesh of your exalted Saviour; and ye go on after your own. Time's thread's shorter by an inch than it was. An oath is sworn and past the seals; whether afflictions will or will not, ye must grow, and swell out of your shell, and live, and triumph and reign, and be more than a conqueror. For your Captain who leadeth you on is more than conqueror and He maketh you partaker of His conquest and victory."

—SAMUEL RUTHERFORD.

THE word "paradise" is used by Paul as equivalent to the third heaven, the abode of God. So also the word paradise is used in Revelation, "To him that overcometh will I give to eat of the tree of Life which grows in the midst of the paradise of God."

Paradise is a place separated, distinguished, emphasized as a marked and distinct place, and as a place of eminent distinction and beauty,—as the abode of God and the angelic beings, and to which true Christians will be taken after death. God's paradise—how matchless its beauty! How unparalleled in every excellence, dignity and loveliness it must be! To that the thief was to be translated—to be translated that day—gracious home to him when that jeering and infuriated mob took him

59

out that his cross might defame and cast equal
odium on that of the Son of God. How, instead
of increasing the ignominy and shame of Jesus, it
added to the luster and power of that cross by lifting a robber from the shame and guilt of the cross
to the glorious beauties of heaven! "To-day shalt
thou be with me in paradise," has given hope of
immortality to many a sinner as he has lifted his
prayerful, dying eyes, and said, "Remember me."

Heaven is a place of rarest beauty and purity,
but the sinful robbers go there, washed in the blood
of the Lamb. "*With me*"—what exalted glory,
supreme dignity, divine companionship, for a
thief! How close the union, how infinite the con-
descension of Jesus, to be the companion, and to
share His glory and joy with him! One of the
noblest memorials to the death of Jesus is that
thief lifted from the cross of guilt to a throne of
glory. The wonders of that death! What tongue
can tell of its marvels, what imagination discover
its miracles! This is one of them. "To-day shalt
thou be with me in paradise," but that is only the
beginning, the index printing to its untold volumes.

In the notable conversation Jesus had with
Nicodemus, the position to which He will elevate
all who believe in Him is denominated "eternal
life."

"And as Moses lifted up the serpent in the wilder-
ness, even so must the Son of man be lifted up; that
whosoever believeth in him should not perish, but

have eternal life. For God so loved the world, that he gave his only begotten Son, that whosoever believeth in him should not perish, but have everlasting life " (John 3: 15–16).

And again, in the fourth chapter (v. 36), the eternal glory is designated as eternal life, and it is the harvest of our faithful patient sowing and tilling in this life. "And he that reapeth, receiveth wages, and gathereth fruit unto life eternal; that both he that soweth and he that reapeth may rejoice together."

The resurrection is unto life:

" Marvel not at this: for the hour is coming, in the which all that are in the graves shall hear his voice, And shall come forth; they that have done good, unto the resurrection of life; and they that have done evil, unto the resurrection of damnation " (John 5: 28).

That wonderful saying to Martha is the declaration of the same great truth that the crowning glory of the future is eternal life:

"Jesus said unto her, Thy brother shall rise again. Martha saith unto him, I know that he shall rise again in the resurrection at the last day. Jesus said unto her, I am the resurrection, and the life: he that believeth in me, though he were dead, yet shall he live: And whosoever liveth and believeth in me shall never die. Believest thou this? She said unto him, Yea, Lord: I believe that thou art the Christ, the

Son of God, which should come into the world"
(John 2:23–27).

So also we hear Jesus say:

"He that loveth his life shall lose it, and he that
hateth his life in this world shall keep it unto life
eternal" (John 12:25).

We come to that magnificent comforting promise which Jesus gave to His disciples among His
last talks with them before His death, while the
gloom of Gethsemane and Calvary was on them
and on Him:

"Let not your heart be troubled: ye believe in
God, believe also in me. In my Father's house are
many mansions: if it were not so, I would have told
you. I go to prepare a place for you. And if I
go and prepare a place for you, I will come again,
and receive you unto myself; that where I am, there
ye may be also" (John 14:1–3).

Heaven will relieve all the troubles of this life.
Every earthly pain is to be eased, all fiery trials
quenched, all tears dried by heaven. Jesus in this
statement makes heaven a place; "I go to prepare
a *place* for you. If I go and prepare a *place* for
you—where I am"—Jesus is local, and located in
heaven. There ye may be also. Somewhere in
God's house of many mansions does Jesus hold
sway, sit up on His throne, and manifest His glory.
There with their exalted Lord, His saints dwell in

eternal, unalloyed good. We cannot fail to see not
only the purpose and inflexible decree of Jesus to
have us in His Father's house, but also the longings of His heart: " Where I am, there ye may be
also,"—an announcement of association and eternal union in felicity, honor and power.

This comes out most fully in His sacerdotal
prayer: " Father, I will that they also whom thou
hast given me, be with me where I am, that they
may behold my glory, which thou hast given me."
Not idle speculations of that glory, but sharers as
well as seers of that glory. That Jesus wants us
with Him, is not a mere sentiment, to adorn or
sweeten, but it is a declared, operative, and eternal
decree, " Father *I will.*" His heart and authority
are in it.

" I have the desire to depart and be with Christ
which is far better," says Paul. To be in heaven,
is to be with Christ, " at home with the Lord."

That Jesus has " gone to heaven to appear in
the presence of God for us," is true, and that by
the mystery and ministry of His death, and the
glory and wealth of His intercession, He is preparing a place for us and preparing us for the
place, is also true.

Jesus is exalted in heaven at the right hand of
the throne of God. The throne is the symbol of
power, and the right hand the symbol of honor,
glory, and majesty. So Jesus is exalted to the
highest place in heaven to which God's power can

raise Him. The apostle declares the exalted dignity of Jesus thus: " According to the working of his mighty power, which he wrought in Christ, when he raised him from the dead, and set him at his own right hand in the heavenly places, far above all principalities, and power, and might, and dominion, and every name that is named, not only in this world, but also in that which is to come: And hath put all things under his feet, and gave him to be the head over all things to the church; which is his body, the fulness of him that filleth all in all."

The highest position of legal glory is His, and we are to be with Him and share His place, and be partners with Him in all the splendors and emoluments of the eternal world. With what divine munificence and magnificence does God crown, exalt and glorify Jesus! So with the same exhaustless munificence and magnificence the Son dispenses to His glorified ones the boundless wealth of heaven.

What Jesus has done for us here in the startling and extravagant advent of Himself into this world, His humiliation and suffering unparalleled in the annals of time and of eternity,—these are the true mirrors of the wonderful, unspeakable, and indescribable things which He will do for us in the other world, but only the faint reflection of them. For His ability is much increased, and the conditions far more favorable there, for Him to do for us than when under the limitations which fettered Him here.

What will be the material blessings and settings of that heavenly life, we cannot tell, but that they will be of the purest and most exquisite form and material, we may be well assured, and of the most reposeful and rapture-giving kind.

Of one thing we are constantly reminded, that Jesus will be with us and will serve us ever like a shepherd feeding his flock, on the richest and best food of heaven, and leading us even to new and living fountains of bliss and knowledge and light. To have Jesus with us will be the acme and sum of all happiness, of all perfection, of all good. What beauty in His face! What wealth untold in His character! How illimitable His resources to bless, eternity only can unfold.

This Christ, what matchless, indescribable charms has He here for those who are possessed of His love. The gifted and saintly Samuel Rutherford while in prison, overflowing with love, uses his great gifts, which by his great love are turned to poetry, to speak of Jesus and His loveliness:

"I never believed till now that there was so much to be found in Christ on this side death and heaven. Oh, the ravishments of heavenly joy which may be had here, in the small gleanings and comforts that fall from Christ."

If Jesus was so much to the gifted and holy Samuel Rutherford, while banished and a prisoner

and in this world, what must He be to those in
heaven? What ineffable beauties must there be in
the unfoldings of His character to the glorified!
What a heaven it must be! It cannot be said too
strongly we are bound to love heaven for Jesus'
sake. We are bound to long for heaven because
Jesus is there. We are bound to be filled with
transportation joy when the hour comes to go
there, because it is the hour to see Jesus, the hour
to meet Jesus, the hour to enjoy Jesus, and to enjoy
Him forever, the hour to be with Him and to be
with Him forever.

> O Paradise, O Paradise,
>   Who doth not crave for rest?
> Who would not seek the happy land
>   Where they that loved are blest;
>
> Where loyal hearts and true,
>   Stand ever in the light,
> All rapture, through and through
>   In God's most holy sight?
>
> O Paradise! O Paradise!
>   The world is growing old;
> Who would not be at rest and free
>   Where love is never cold?

V

HEAVEN AND ETERNAL LIFE

"After it was noised about that Mr. Valiant—for truth was taken with a summons by the same post as the other, and had this for a token that the summons was true, that 'his pitcher was broken at the fountain.' When he understood it he called for his friends and told them of it. Then said he, 'I am going to my Father's and though with great difficulty I got hither yet now I do not repent me of all the trouble I have been at to arrive where I am.' When the day that he must go over was come many accompanied him to the river-side, into which as he went he said, 'Death, where is thy sting? Grave, where is thy victory?' So he passed over, and all the trumpets sounded for him on the other side."

—John Bunyan.

THE Bible makes much use of the term life as the central and fundamental idea of heaven, its enjoyments, employments and character. The term is almost too literal to be reckoned as a symbol. It is a most comprehensive symbol, and its nearness to the literal but enhances its value as a symbol.

The New Testament abounds in the use of this symbol. It is the sum and results of the Gospel. Faith plants the seed of eternal life in the heart, and it germinates and grows in the faithful heart through all the struggles and years of this life, but

67

it finds its eternal unfolding in fullest expansion and amplitude in heaven. "As many as were ordained to eternal life."

"To them who by patient continuance in well doing seek for glory and honor and immortality, eternal life" (Rom. 2: 7).

"Shall reign in life by one Jesus Christ."

"That as sin hath reigned unto death, even so might grace reign through righteousness unto eternal life by Jesus Christ our Lord" (Rom. 5: 21).

"Reign in life!" What is that? This: "But now being made free from sin, and become servants to God, ye have your fruit unto holiness, and the end everlasting life. For the wages of sin is death; but the gift of God is eternal life through Jesus Christ our Lord."

Paul in giving the reason why the true Christian groans to enter into heaven, says, "For we that are in this tabernacle do groan being burdened, not for that we would be unclothed, but clothed upon, that mortality might be swallowed up of life."

To Timothy, Paul says, "Lay hold on eternal life whereunto thou art called." The rich he exhorts in this wise:

"That they do good, that they be rich in good works, ready to distribute, willing to communicate; Laying up in store for themselves a good foundation against the time to come, that they may lay hold on eternal life" (1 Tim. 6: 18–19).

James designates heaven as a " crown of life." It is called " the resurrection of life." The statements of the apostles and Christ with this symbol of heaven life, eternal life, implies that it is an eternal freedom from and opposition to death. In the term life is concentrated every good which man can desire to enjoy. " Heaven is the possession, in the highest sense, of the first and last blessing of man, which has been well said to be the essence of all happiness." Life is the state and affluence of heaven—immortal life, undecayed and undecaying, with no liability to decay or diminution. The state, environments and advances of the heavenly world are all life, more life, deeper, wider, sweeter life. Its book is the Book of life; its crowns of life are crowning; its river, the river of life; its tree, the tree of life; its water, the water of life.

It was the all engrossing question of the young man who came to Jesus, " What shall I do that I may inherit eternal life?" How attractive and charmful this life! What a divine gift is this life! It is bounded by the cradle, the symbol of helplessness and want, and by death, the impersonation of all that is dark, painful, and terrific. Enfeebled by disease, hampered by sickness, and marred by sore distress, with severe struggles, sad disappointments, yet to it we cling, for it we toil, and at last surrender it only in a despairing or triumphant struggle.

But eternal life involves the untold, unimagined

and fadeless glories of heaven! What measureless wealth! What deathless raptures! What glorious intoxication! No description dare attempt its picture! The most exalted strains of music would be discord to the harmony of heaven and all brightest visions would turn into darkest midnight! All summer suns would chill like the ice of December when contrasted with the splendor of its nightless day. The most gifted, exalted and sweetest poetry of earth would be but dull prose in heaven. What is eternal life? Who can dream or imagine that life? Heaven has it! Heaven holds it! as the surprise of the saints as they leave earth and pass through the gates of the celestial city.

Jesus is said to lead the heavenly inhabitants to " fountains of living water." In this we have the figure of life, ever new and continuous. Here is a life that refreshes, blesses and satisfies the soul as water refreshes, blesses and satisfies the body. Here is a constant unfolding of life, life to the full and overflowing, like a fountain, new discoveries of life, its hidden sources opened up, ever new, ever fresh.

Heaven will be the pursuit of life, the employment of life, the enjoyment of life, the increase of life. Its pursuits, its employment and its enjoyment will be eternal. Life in heaven will be a rapture, a bliss untold. All the man, mind, soul and spirit, will be widened and elevated, deepened, refined and beautified by it. Everything will con-

spire to make that life supremely blest and supremely glorious. Christ will feed that life on
richest pasturage. Christ will lead that life to
fountains of living water. " God will wipe away
all tears " from the eyes of that life.

> The heavens shall glow with splendor,
>   But brighter far than they
> The saints shall shine in glory,
>   As Christ shall them array:
> The beauty of the Saviour,
>   Shall dazzle every eye,
>   In the crowning day that's coming by and by.
>
> Our pain shall then be over,
>   We'll sin and sigh no more;
> Behind us all of sorrow,
>   And naught but joy before,
> A joy in our Redeemer,
>   As we to him are nigh,
>   In the crowning day that's coming by and by.

VI

HEAVEN AND THE HOLY SPIRIT

" The eye of flesh is not capable of seeing, nor the ear of hearing, nor the heart of understanding heaven and its glories. But there the eye, the ear, and the heart are made capable. Else how could we enjoy those things in heaven? The more perfect the sight, the more delightful will be the beautiful object. The more perfect the appetite, the sweeter the food; the more musical the ear, the more pleasant the melody, and the more perfect the soul, the more joyous these joys, and the more glorious these glories."
—RICHARD BAXTER.

THE Holy Spirit, in us, is said to be " the earnest of heaven." The " earnest " is the security and foretaste, and so the Holy Spirit is the certainty of heaven and its foretaste. He puts the fact of heaven, the taste of heaven, the power of heaven and the ambition and toil for heaven, freshly, strongly and constantly in our hearts. The refrain and chorus are, " Heaven is my home."

" In whom ye also trusted, after that ye heard the word of truth, the gospel of your salvation; in whom also after that ye believed, ye were sealed with the Holy Spirit of promise. Which is the earnest of our inheritance until the redemption of the purchased

possession, unto the praise of his glory" (Ephes.
1:13).

"Now he which establishes us with you in Christ,
and hath anointed us is God, who hath also sealed us,
and given the earnest of the Spirit in our hearts"
(2 Cor. 1:21).

What do these great texts mean? They present
to us the ministry and work of the Holy Spirit as
He forms in us the fact and experience of heaven,
and shapes us in desire and in heavenliness, and in
heavenly longings and heavenly fashion, at every
point.

The music and hope of heaven would fill and
sweeten our lives if we lived in the full power of
the Spirit. What transporting anticipations!
What "joy unspeakable and full of glory" would
brighten our living and our dying days! The
Spirit's power settles our faith, and quickens the
sentiment about heaven. By the Spirit's mighty
workings, heaven becomes an assured, a sublime
and a glorious fact. The power of the Holy Spirit
puts us on the stretch for the good world, and puts
in us a thirst for heaven. He gives us constant and
enlarged tastes and visions of heaven, till all other
tastes pall and all other visions are heavy and dull.
He gives us notes of its harmony and all earth's
notes are discord. The power of the Spirit binds
us to heaven because Jesus is there. We are bound
to love it, think about it and be ravished by it, for
Jesus is its center and glory.

How strongly and insistently does the Holy Spirit use heaven and its untold and manifold good to move saints to action, to awaken from death, to make zeal hot and love ardent. The Holy Spirit implants heaven in us. The Holy Spirit Himself, given to us, is God's mark of ownership and security. His authority is put on us. But it is not His sealing process, its condition, significance, or results in full, with which we have to do now, but of one phase, the *earnest* of future and eternal things. The Holy Spirit is the earnest of heaven to us. "Earnest" means the pledge which, in purchase, is given that the contract will be faithfully and fully carried out. An earnest is part of the thing itself, given as a security that the whole will be given in its time. Through the Holy Spirit God gives us a part of heaven as a pledge of the full heaven when the time is ripe. The Holy Spirit is to us both a foretaste and a pledge of heaven. The first instalment of heaven is given by the Holy Spirit.

The Holy Spirit makes much of heaven. He is Himself to us "the earnest," the pledge and foretaste of heaven. He puts heaven in us when He puts Himself in us, and all our tastes, struggles, relishes and longings for heaven are the creations of His power and the sure tests of His presence. If there be no heavenly lookings, no heavenly spirit, no heavenly yearnings in us, there is no Holy Spirit in us. God works in us a fitness for

the heavenly world by the Holy Spirit and plants in
us the heavenly mind and the heavenly image.
The indwelling Spirit of God makes us unlike earth
and like heaven. The Holy Spirit matures hope
to its brightest luster, and enables the saint to
" glory in tribulation " and " rejoice in hope of
the glory of God."

Paul, by the spirit, made much of heaven. In
his mid-career, fastened to life and earth by his
strenuous toil, he pauses lest his unremitting toil
should earthen him, and he records his loyalty to
heaven and to Jesus, for in Paul's estimation, and
in every true estimate, they are one. " I am in a
strait betwixt two, having a desire to depart and
be with Christ which is far better." We find him
on the stretch always for heaven, always " confident and willing rather to be absent from the
body and to be at home with the Lord." He is
ever pressing on: " Forgetting the things that are
behind, and reaching forth to those things that are
before, I press toward the mark for the prize of
my high calling of God in Christ Jesus." He is
always " keeping his body under, and keeping it in
subjection," that he might not lose the incorruptible
crown. At the close, his good battle fought, his
course finished, the faith kept, heaven is still in
full view, its crown gleaming brighter under Nero's
axe. It is the thought, the hope, the fact of heaven
which forms Christian character and matures it
into its unearthly beauty and perfection.

The stimulating demands of entering into eternal life could not be set forth with more terrific colorings and imperative exactions than by Jesus Christ. "If thy hand cause thee to stumble cut it off: it is good for thee to enter into life maimed, rather than having two hands to go into hell, into the unquenchable fire."

Heaven is termed a reward. "Great is your reward in heaven," says Christ to His persecuted and reviled disciples. And so in Revelation: "And behold, I come quickly; and my reward is with me, to give every man according as his work shall be." The meaning is dues paid for work. "For the Son of man shall come in the glory of his Father with his angels; and then he shall reward every man according to his works."

> Then let the wildest storms arise;
> Let tempests mingle earth and skies;
> No fatal shipwrecks shall I fear,
> But all my treasures with me bear.
>
> If thou, my Jesus, still be nigh,
> Cheerful I live, and joyful die;
> Secure, when mortal comforts flee,
> To find ten thousand worlds in thee.
> —*Philip Doddridge.*

VII

HEAVEN, A STATE

"And I heard as it were the voice of a great multitude . . . saying, Hallelujah! for the Lord our God the Almighty reigneth. Let us rejoice and be exceeding glad, for the marriage of the Lamb is come and His wife hath made herself ready."—REVELATION 19 : 6.

HEAVEN is *a state* as well as a place. Whatever the outward appearance may be, however entrancing to eye, how fascinating to ear, how pleasing to taste or touch, how ecstatic to feeling all the scenes and sounds, enjoyments and felicities may be, these are not the prime sources of its attraction. It is *a state*—a state of enthronement, elevation and freedom. It is emancipation. Much has been left behind of the old, the worn out and the burdensome, and much of new, the strange and the wonderful will be there. It will be a state of *perfected knowledge*. Then we shall know even as we are known. God knows us perfectly here. We will know Him and all things perfectly there.

"For we know in part, and we prophesy in part. But when that which is perfect is come, then that which is in part shall be done away. When I was a child, I spake as a child, I understood as a child, I thought as a child: but when I became a man, I put away childish things. For now we see through a glass, darkly; but then face to face: now I know in part; but then shall I know even as also I am known" (1 Cor. 13:9–12).

What will be the unspeakable benefactions in a state when we know all things perfectly! Neither height nor depth, nor breadth, nor length, in heaven and earth and hell that will not lie open to our knowledge in that exalted and perfected state where all mysteries will be gone.

In the sixth chapter of Romans we have a statement vital to heaven: "But now being made free from sin, and become servants to God, ye have your fruit unto holiness, and the end everlasting life." To "make free" is to emancipate. The negroes are free, no slavish chains enthrall them. A dual action is here seen. There is emancipation from sin and enslavement to God—an attitude of repulsion, of entire freedom from sin, and an attitude of entire enslavement to God. These bear the fruit of holiness if found in a heart where God reigns, from which sin is excluded. To such a state and to such a character heaven belongs by heirship, by right. Two struggles mark the true heavenly life—to be freed from sin, to be wholly devoted to God.

How free can I be from sin? How thoroughly devoted to God can I be? These are questions which have engaged and often perplexed the holiest of men. Too much time and thought have been given to these trying by theoretical or verbal statement to fix the limits. The Scriptures make strong affirmations at this point. The holy Boardman in Burmah says:

"I find on reading the apostles' writings that they address their fellow Christians and speak of themselves as persons that are dead to sin, buried with Christ into death. They are dead, and their lives are hid with Christ in God. They have crucified the flesh with its affections and lusts. Their old man is crucified with Christ. They are dead to sin by consequence and are freed from sin. They cease from sin. Being born of God, they sin not, they cannot sin, they have overcome the world, the world is crucified to them and they to the world.

"Now these things are mentioned not only as things to be desired or sought after, but as already obtained. 'Ye are dead—have crucified the flesh —have put off the old man—are freed from sin— hath ceased from sin.'"

Thus queried this man of God. How many before and since have raised the same questions? Of one thing we may be sure that the experience and attitude of Christian attainment and obtainment set forth in the New Testament is open to all Christians of every age and every clime. Books on holiness may give us no light and theories may con-

fuse. But with our Bible before us and the open
door of prayer, and the increasing light and power
of the Holy Spirit, each can settle the question as
a personal experience, keeping the divine statement
ever before the mind, " Free from sin and become
the servants of God," emancipation from sin most
complete, enslavement to God most perfect, with
the full possibilities of God's grace, Christ's blood,
the power of the Holy Spirit and of faith—that
God is " able to do exceeding abundantly above all
that we ask or think "—that all things are possible
to him that believeth—that " He that spared not
his own Son but delivered him up for us all, how
shall he not with him freely give us all things? "—
that God has given us all things in Christ—that by
prayer we can have all that there is in Christ—that
we are charged to " be filled with all the fulness of
God "—that God is able to make us abound in all
grace—that " always having all sufficiency in all
things may abound to every good work "—that
God can " make us perfect in every good work to
do his will, working in us that which is well pleasing in his sight "—that God can make us, " that
we may stand perfect and complete in all the will
of God." All these wonderful and far-reaching
Scriptural statements concerning the possibilities
of grace, fully answer the question as to how free
we can be from sin and how thoroughly we can be
devoted to God.

This " fruit unto holiness " is absolutely necessary as a prerequisite for heaven. "Without holiness no man shall see the Lord." Holiness is an imperative, inflexible, eternal condition of heaven. A holy God, a holy Jesus, a holy heaven, demand holiness among men as well as among angels. "Every man that striveth for masteries is temperate in all things. They do it to obtain a corruptible crown, but we an incorruptible. I therefore so run not as uncertainly, so fight I, not as one that beateth the air: But I keep under my body and bring it into subjection; lest that by any means when I have preached to others I myself should be a castaway." So writes Paul to the Corinthians.

The heavenly-fitting virtue here stressed is that of temperance, self-control, the strong master of self under the law of strict self-denial. The apostle enforces the necessity of temperance by reference to the athlete who spent much time in training, and who denied himself of those things which were agreeable and in which they ordinarily indulged. Their training, temperance and strict self-denial were familiar and emphasized this virtue in a strong way. It is heaven of which the apostle is writing, and the presence of this temperance in all things, this self-control, was not only to be exercised in the higher realms of man's nature, but the Christian's bodily appetites were to feel the strong hand of this temperance. Not simply to become Christians was it necessary, but its daily and hourly exercise were necessary to continue Chris-

tians. Without it the highest range of Christian
elevation and obtainment would keep one from be-
coming a reprobate. "I keep under my body"
means to strike heavily in the face so as to render
black and blue a hard subject, so as to reduce it
to self-control, and also bring the body into subjection and enslave it. "The body is the adversary considered as the seat of the temptations of
Satan, and especially that of self-indulgence."

By self-control the pride, obstinacy and self-
seeking appetites are to be restrained and broken
down. The flesh and spirit are to be brought under the law of this heavenly race. No one is free
from this law. The apostle declares elsewhere:
"He that striveth for the mastery is not crowned
except he strive lawfully." An examination of the
victors in the combats took place after the contest,
and if it were found that the race had been won
by unlawful means they were deprived of the prize.
The law for the heavenly contestants is severe self-
control. Without it all seeming success in the
heavenly race will be rejected and discrowned.

Heaven makes redemption full, the purchase
complete, the possession perfect, the pledge sure.
Even here we have the foretaste of the full heaven.
Heaven is joy unmixed, eternal, rapturous. Here
we have by the presence of the Holy Spirit, "joy
unspeakable and full of glory." Even here we
"rejoice evermore," "rejoice always." To rejoice
is the command of earth as well as the luxury of

heaven. Heaven is the place and state of perfect rest, but even here by the Holy Spirit peace reigns. Our " peace flows as a river." " The peace of God which passeth all understanding shall keep your hearts and your minds in Christ Jesus." This is the type and beginning of heaven's peace. The kingdom of God in this world is " Righteousness, Peace, and Joy in the Holy Ghost." The kingdom of God in the next world will be but the perfection of righteousness, peace, and joy. " The redemption of the purchased possession " is changed in the Revised Version to, " Unto the redemption of God's own possession." God's possession of us is by the Holy Spirit, not by redemption, not by being bought back only, but by God taking possession of us, by yielding ourselves to be filled, possessed, controlled, owned by God, mastered absolutely by God. He is to have unlimited authority over us and supreme unmixed control in us. That is God's rule here, the precursor and earnest of His reign in the better world. Heaven will give us fullest possession of God, and heaven will give God the fullest possession of us. But heaven is only for those who are God's possession here.

God's Word reveals another land where the misfortune of poverty and the curse of crime never come, where a life of beggary and a death of the cross puts no stigma on character, no mark on the brow, no ostracism. Heaven is made up of the outlaws of earth, of earth's banished ones.

Here is Scriptural description of such characters as will be found in heaven:

" They had trials of cruel mockings, and scourgings, yea, moreover of bonds and imprisonment: They were stoned, they were sawn asunder, were tempted, were slain with the sword: they wandered about in sheepskins and goatskins; being destitute, afflicted, tormented (of whom the world was not worthy); they wandered in deserts, and in mountains, and in dens and caves of the earth " (Heb. 11: 36).

Wonderful grace which makes saints and immortals of earth's defamed and ostracized ones!

Wonderful association and companionship for our Lord, the beggar Lazarus and all holy beggars who have learned by their begging the secret of faith and who have the heart for heaven! Wonderful companionship and association for our adorable and Divine Lord—a thief banned by earthly justice to the cross! wonderful power of that death to make the redeemed and glorious ones of heaven out of the refuse of earth, out of its beggarly crime! Glorious companionship of a beggar and robber to be with our Lord in Paradise! Royal exaltation and renown, to add to the glory of Himself and to the renown of Abraham, by making Lazarus, earth's ostracized one, his own companion! How the false estimates, false reputations, false rewards of earth are reversed and rectified in Christ's heaven!

In the parable of the rich man and Lazarus Jesus teaches us much of heaven as well as many sad and alarming lessons of hell. All men do not go to heaven. All men *might* go to heaven, but all men will not go to heaven. This we learn from the rich man, who in hell lifted up his eyes being in torments. Heaven is not subjected to the financial and social influences of this world. Lazarus the beggar has no money, no friends, no social influence. He has committed the unpardonable crime of earth, of being a beggar. He is ostracized, friendless, lives without money, dies without friends and is buried without tears. But heaven—who can understand it? It receives Lazarus, the beggar on earth, into more than kingly society; angels are his attendants, and he becomes the bosom friend and associate of Abraham, the rich man, the " friend of God," peerless in social elevation. Heavenly society is not based on money nor any of its tributaries, incidents or accidents. Purity of character reigns in heaven, but money does not.

The favorite Bible word for heaven is " glory," which seems so especially suited to describe heaven. It means splendor, brightness, magnificence, excellence, preëminence, dignity, majesty in the sense of absolute perfection, a most glorious, a most exalted state, a glorious condition of blessedness.

A *happy* state heaven will be. There might be perfection in knowledge and not bliss. There might be progress and pain. There might be glory, effulgence and splendor, which would bring no calm to the breast, no joy to the heart. But heaven's state will be one of supreme, unalloyed happiness, with nothing to shadow its brightness, nothing to bring pain, or cause sorrow. There is ineffable joy, no void, no fear, no anxiety, no alloy.

There are real joys in heaven. We are not apprised of their pursuits, their high vocations, but neither listlessness nor weariness will be known. Activity is the first and strongest impression given us of heaven, an activity too intense and profound to be intermitted or to be joyless. Their joys are of the highest and most engaging order, no fitful delights, no dreamy visions, but filling the heart, the mind, and the spirit.

We can, perhaps, more readily appreciate its joys by negative statement than by the positive, by the ills we shall escape, as fully, or more so, than by the joys we shall inherit:

"No sickness." What an immeasurable bliss! "No pain." What endless comfort and ease! "No sorrow," no cloud, no night, no weariness, no bitterness, no anguish, no penitence, no remorse, no graves, no sighs, no tears, no sad laments, no broken hearts, no death-bed scenes, no dying there. Never a corpse, never a coffin, never a hearse, never a grave in all that happy, thrice blissful land. No funeral crowd ever wept, no sorrowing ones ever pass through its streets, or walk along its cloudless highways. Not only is there an absence of these things, which destroy earth's brightest bliss. Their absence is enough to form a delightful heaven. But there is positive good, " fulness of joy and pleasures forevermore."

> No chilling winds, or poisonous breath,
>   Can reach that healthful shore;
> Sickness and sorrow, pain and death,
>   Are felt and feared no more.
>
> When shall I reach that happy place,
>   And be forever blest?
> When shall I see my Father's face,
>   And in his bosom rest?

VIII

GRACES WHICH FIT FOR HEAVEN

" The soul is renewed in the glory world. The body will
be fashioned after the glorious body of Jesus Christ, and
both will be joined together in an indestructible bond,
clearer than the indestructible Moon, brighter than the Sun,
and more resplendent than all the heavenly spheres. For
having conquered and triumphed in the church militant, the
saint is now sit down with Jesus on His throne. Hallelujah!
The Lord God omnipotent reigneth. And His children
shall reign with Him forever.

" An unholy man cannot enter heaven, and were he in
heaven, it would be no enjoyment to him, because it is not
suited to him. The nature of resident must be suited to the
place of residence. . . . There is a fellowship among the
devils in hell, and with those who are of a diabolic nature,
and we know that holy inhabitants of heaven are brethren
with holy souls."

—ADAM CLARK.

THE results of Paul's profound and matchless argument on the resurrection of the
body and its transfiguration for the
heavenly world, is summarized and pointed thus:
" Therefore, my beloved brethren, be ye steadfast,
unmovable, always abounding in the work of the
Lord, for as much as ye know that your labor is not
in vain in the Lord." That is to be settled, fixed
in purpose, not moved, firmly persistent, settled to

stay. Of King Rehoboam it is said, " He did evil because he set not his heart to seek the Lord " (Revised Version). " He that wavereth is like a wave of the sea, driven with the wind and tossed. For let not that man think that he shall receive anything of the Lord. A double-minded man is unstable in all his ways." Instability loses heaven. " My heart is fixed, oh God, my heart is fixed." That is, his heart was seated, settled, immovable for heaven. No one goes to heaven whose heart is not already there.

Perseverance is a heaven-winning grace, to be at it always, to stay at it all the time. The king of Israel lost his conquest because he smote on the ground but three times when he should have smitten twice that number. He missed by stopping. We miss heaven by not persevering. Faint-heartedness, or weariness and letting go, are fatal conditions in the ascent to heaven. " And let us not be weary in well doing, for in due season we shall reap, if we faint not." It takes strength to gain heaven. They need strong men there. They are strong who gain heaven. Much there will be in this life to create faint-heartedness and much to discourage. To hold on will require resolute fortitude and persevering courage and steady ongoing.

The ability to die is a heaven-gaining virtue. Paul says, " I die daily." He wanted his dying fashioned after the perfect pattern of Christ.

" Conformed to his death." " I am crucified with Christ: nevertheless I live; yet not I, but Christ liveth in me: and the life which I now live in the flesh I live by the faith of the Son of God, who loved me, and gave himself for me." Again the apostle says: " But God forbid that I should glory, save in the cross of our Lord Jesus Christ, by whom the world is crucified unto me, and I unto the world."

Along the heavenly way the cross is to be borne. The cross is the true sign that we are in the heavenly way. As Jesus bore the cross, so must all His true disciples do the same. As Jesus died on the cross to save from sin, so must we die to sin, to self and to the world, a painful death, but it is the crowning death. As Jesus went to His Father's right hand from the cross, so we go to His right hand by way of the cross. If no shame of the cross, no joys of the crown. If no death of the cross, no life of the crown. If no depression of the cross, no elevation of the throne. " It is a faithful saying: For if we be dead with him, we shall also live with him; If we suffer, we shall also reign with him; if we deny him he also will deny us."

In the first chapter of second Peter we have a catalogue of the heavenly-fitting graces! " And besides this, giving all diligence, add to your faith virtue; and to virtue, knowledge; and to knowledge, temperance; and to temperance, patience; and to patience, godliness; and to godliness, brotherly kindness; and to brotherly kindness, charity."

The apostle has been writing of the wonderful provision God had made for our salvation. "According as his divine power hath given unto us all things that pertain unto life and godliness, through the knowledge of him that hath called us to glory and virtue; whereby are given unto us exceeding great and precious promises; that by these ye might be partakers of the divine nature, having escaped the corruption that is in the world through lust."

We have in this statement a summary of God's great outlay, laid out, laid down before us, and we are to contribute, besides what God has done, our quota, or, as the Revised Version says: "Yea and for this very cause adding on your part all diligence," introducing by the side of God's great works, all diligence. In all things concerning heaven, diligence is a necessary virtue. Sustained, persevering, deeply interested effort, is a matter of vital importance. Sloth and ease, so criminal and so ensnaring in every department of earthly action and effort, are peculiarly so in the effort for heaven. Not to be in earnest about heaven—here is a crime of great magnitude, eternal in fatal consequences. At the very threshold of the way to heaven, we are confronted with the fact that he who would win eternal life must be deeply in earnest, and express that earnestness by most laborious and persistent effort. To this struggle for heaven, every contestant must bring all diligence at the outset. Through all the way till the heavenly gates are entered, there can be no slacking of diligence. This diligence is to be put forth to bring to being and perfection all the graces which fit for heaven.

Faith is the first, the foundation stone. Faith builds on Jesus Christ. Here faith is the foundation on which the whole spiritual building is reared. A foundation will do no good and will be ruined if no house is built on it. The snow, the rain, the dew, the frost, the air, the sunshine, the breeze, will dissolve a foundation of adamant if no house be built on it. On faith's foundation, by all diligence, the spiritual superstructure must be reared. The word " add " is taken from the leader of a chorus, which means to bring forward and supply all things necessary to fit out the chorus. We are to add all things requisite to make the heavenly character complete and harmonious.

Virtue is to be added. Virtue is an eminent endowment, a combination of all virtues, at least of many of them. In this place it means vigor, manly vigor, made of all manly qualities. Courage is a chief and distinguishing idea in virtue. *Knowledge* is general understanding and intelligence, that knowledge of Jesus and Divine things which instruct. It involves the intelligent apprehension of Divine truths and a thorough conviction of their importance. This knowledge is gained in the Holy

Bible and by the light of God's Spirit. We are to seek the Spirit of revelation in the knowledge of Jesus. More and more are we to know of Jesus. More and more are we to " know Him and the power of His resurrection." Knowledge is power and strength and light. We are to be deeply convicted of the truths of religion, and must have a personal knowledge of what the Scriptures teach, and an intelligent grasp and apprehension of Bible facts and truths. Light and wisdom in the inner man—all these are to be added day by day as the lessons for heaven's graduating day.

Temperance follows, and this word is not limited in its meaning to intoxicants. It means self-government. We have learned of ourselves by knowledge. Self-control comes in to bear its fruit of heavenly wisdom. The tempers and passions, appetites and desires, are all held in by the strong reins of temperance. It cannot be that intemperance can enter heaven. Desires are to be limited, as well as appetites and passion. A passionless man may be in excess through his desires after money, after business success and after pleasures. Self-governed for God—this expresses its meaning. Trained in the school of temperance for heaven—this is the idea.

Patience comes to prominence again, and combines with these other graces to perfect in us the Christian character and fit us for the heavenly life. In this noble word there is always a background of manliness. It is the brave patience with which the Christian contends against the various hindrances, persecutions and temptations which befall him in his conflict with the inner self and outer world. It is that manliness which never loses heart or courage, never charges God foolishly, and is not hasty nor revengeful to man.

Godliness, God-likeness, brings the heavenly racer into a heavenly atmosphere. He is no longer simply after virtue, knowledge, temperance, patience, which are principles, facts, restraints, but after the pattern of a person. He is looking heavenward for a pattern after which to shape his conduct and character. He hears the law speaking through the soft tunes of the Gospel, " Be ye holy for I am holy." It is God who speaks, and the struggle for heaven reaches its brightest point when it begins to be a struggle to be like God. Higher relations than earth bind him, higher duties than those to man. He is rising to God. He is struggling for God's perfect image, that he may be a reflection of the Divine Person.

He has passed into the Divine family. His relation to God gives him a new kinship to man. Love is to rule in a family circle. A brotherhood has been established, which is the family of God, the brotherhood of heaven. *Brotherly Love* is one of the germs of our conversion to God. One of the elements of the heavenly life. The brotherhood of earth is the type of the brotherhood of heaven.

Grace has many of the natural virtues. It keeps and polishes these. While not exactly transformed, they are burnished and refined, and adorn humanity with a richness not wholly their own. But grace must have its distinctive features which separate it from and elevate it above all other systems. It must be original and unrivaled in its super-excellence.

Paul, in the twelfth chapter of Romans, has a masterly and beautiful presentation of the practical side of piety, its most beautiful side, for in no shape is religion so lovely as when in action. The crowning grace is set forth by Paul in these words: " Be kindly affectionate one to another; in honor preferring one another." This is a costly grace; like the most precious gems, rare and only secured with great labor and cost. Where is this one to be found? Who exemplifies it?

These jewels are found in God's Word readily, they adorn almost every page; but to transfer them to practical life among our fallen and marred race, is the point of chief difficulty. To transplant these sensitive and rare plants, so that they bloom and spread their odor in a strange soil, is a difficult and delicate task. These fine spiritual graces do not seem to be the product of this hurrying age. We value bulk rather than quality. These are the products of the Divine side of our religion, the proofs of its divinity. It must have something above the rude virtues which spring from the soil of humanity. These heaven-induced graces must be seen and felt. The world demands this before it pays its homage. We are not barren of the ordinary graces. It costs but little to fashion them. But these of the first water, how rare!

It is the glory of Christianity not only to present an ideal of the highest type, but to supply practical illustrations.

"In honor preferring one another." This may be fitly termed *the crowning grace*. To put others along side of us, is generous and gracious, but to put them before us, is divine. To halt that they may catch up, would be kindly, but to stop and step aside that others may pass before us in a race for honor and place, is far above nature. To prefer others before ourselves in heart and action, seems to bewilder and dizzy our untried heads. It is too high. We sigh out in despair. We cannot attain to it. But faith says, "I can do all things through Christ who strengthens me." This crowning of others by discrowning self, this refusing that others may receive, is grievous to flesh and blood. Who can receive it? And yet it comes to us as a command, in the form of law. But the New Testament law unfolds the promise, and affords the helps to obedience. We are to do this—put others before ourselves. This is the complete conquest of self, and requires a great victory. He who has gained this is worthy a triumph through the gates into the City! Have we learned this lesson and gained this height? Have we received the crown of this grace? Can we in honor prefer another? Has the reign of ambition ceased, the love of the world been destroyed, and self crucified? The death of all these must enrich the soil ere it can produce this Divine fruit.

It is as if God speaks thus to His people: " You by your unwearied diligence furnish these graces, and I will furnish heaven. You seek these spiritual graces in their abounding fulness, and I will supply to you an abounding entrance into heaven." So to gain heaven hereafter, we must of necessity gain these rich graces here. Heaven grows in the soil of the God-prepared heart. We seek heaven by seeking these heavenly virtues.

Peter in concluding this earnest exhortation, so full of meaning, concerning those graces which fit us for heaven, gives us these words: " For if these things be in you, and abound, they make you that ye shall neither be barren nor unfruitful in the knowledge of our Lord Jesus Christ." To fail in having, in abounding fulness, these heavenly characteristics, is to be blind to eternal matters, and short-sighted about heaven and all the things pertaining to it, and also to lose what we have already obtained. Past forgiveness amounts to nothing if we do not " add to " this initial step the succeeding stages, which mark the way to heaven. " But he that lacketh these things is blind, and cannot see afar off, and hath forgotten that he was purged from his old sins." Again does this homely apostle call us to diligence, ongoing, and the addition of these graces to the sum already secured, as the only safeguard from backsliding and final apostasy. " Wherefore the rather, brethren, give diligence to make your calling and election sure; for if ye do these things, ye shall never fall."

Then with a master stroke he shows the bearing of all this diligence, toil, and the securement of all these divine graces, on heaven: " For so an entrance shall be ministered unto you abundantly into the everlasting kingdom of our Lord and Saviour Jesus Christ." Or, as the Revised Version has it, " For thus shall be richly supplied unto you the entrance into the eternal kingdom of our Lord and Saviour Jesus Christ."

> Let cares like a wild deluge come,
>   And storms of sorrow fall,
> So I but safely reach my home,
>   My God, my heaven, my all.
>
> There I shall bathe my weary soul
>   In seas of heavenly rest,
> And not a wave of trouble roll
>   Across my peaceful breast.
>   —*Isaac Watts.*

IX

LOVE OF JESUS AND HEAVEN

"In heaven we shall live in our own element. We are now as the fish in a vessel of water, only so much as will keep them alive. But what is that to the ocean? We have here a little air let in to afford us breathing, but what is that to the sweet and fresh gales upon Mount Zion? Here we have a beam of the sun to lighten our darkness and a warm ray to keep us from freezing. But there we shall live in the light and be revived by its heat."

—Richard Baxter.

THE Apostle James says: "Blessed is the man that endureth temptation, for when he is tried he shall receive the crown of life which the Lord hath promised to them that love him." The great condition of this great reward, the crown of life, is Love.

It would be impossible to overestimate the importance of love. Christ makes it the aim of the moral code and the fulfilment of all prophecy. It is called the royal law, and is said to be the fulfilling of that law; the bond of perfection, the test of discipleship, the first of the graces, and the shield on the day of judgment.

In the thirteenth of first Corinthians it is pictured, and we gaze and admire, but rarely do we transfer to practical life this the most beautiful of all things, and the most practical too. Love is not faith, though the only medium through which faith works. It is not hope, though it forms the substance which hope colors and brightens. It is the most common thing, and the rarest, often on our lips, but seldom in our hearts, easiest to say and hardest to do.

What is the description as thus given by Paul? It has passion, but neither envy nor jealousy have any place in that pure flame. It is clothed with humility, so that neither vanity nor pride inflate its heart, nor speak from its lips. Unseemly conduct never mars its beauty, nor casts reproach nor suspicion on its fidelity. Self renders his scepter, and claims his rights with modesty, and meekness. It is never provoked to peevish irritation, not insulted to bitterness, and wrath. It does not suspect ill nor avenge wrongs. It is saddened by the triumphs of evil, but rejoicing in the success of truth. It is akin to God in its freedom from hasty and angry excitements, long-suffering, self-restrained to evil but to the good mobile, and everflowing in kindness, usefulness, beneficence.

It has strength to bear, is credulous for good, full of hope and cheer for the best, and waits patiently, serene and gentle, when faith and fortitude and hope have almost failed.

Such is the divine portraiture of this Divine love. Such are the principles on which Christ proposes to reconstruct human nature—sublime principles, sublimer purposes of the Son of God. Out of no other material does He propose to begin and complete His fair and costly building and make His heaven.

Religion is shut up to this one principle. All else is foreign or false. It is the capsheaf, the commandment which completes, aggregates and dominates the whole; burnished, emphatic and pregnant with His life and death. The summary of that life and death is: " Love one another." This is the decalogue revised and completed—the Sinai of Calvary—the law of the Gospel.

Love is the regenerating principle implanted in man's heart by the Holy Ghost, and its perfection is the end for which he is to labor with incessant effort and incessant prayer.

This love to Jesus implanted in the renewed heart has retired earth's most sacred attachments and become the animating force and crown of our earthly lives. " Where I am there ye may be also." " To be at home with the Lord." " To be with Christ which is far better." " Father, I will that those whom thou hast given me be with me where I am."

To love Jesus is to long to be with Him. To love Jesus is to think about Him. To love Jesus is to obey Him, to obey Him readily and implicitly, not feebly and reluctantly. " If ye love me keep my commandments. If ye keep my commandments ye shall abide in my love." The certainty of heaven is assured when we keep Jesus in the center of our hearts, in the center of our lives. He is to be the author of impulse and desire, of effort and action. "Whatsoever ye do in word or deed, do all in the name of the Lord Jesus."

Will you get to heaven? What is Jesus to you? Does He charm you? Does He draw you heavenward? Is it to be with Him that you seek heaven? Is He the fairest flower in all its garden? Is He the rarest and most precious of all its jewels? Is He sweeter than all its songs?

Does He beget the longings for its blissful abodes? Does the desire to see and be with Him stir the profoundest ambition of your soul? Jesus and heaven are bound up together. To love Him with an untold passionate devotion is heaven begun, heaven continued, and heaven ended. Paul says: " I am now ready to be offered, and the time of my departure is at hand. I have fought a good fight, I have finished my course, I have kept the faith. Henceforth there is laid up for me a crown of righteousness, which the Lord, the righteous judge, shall give me at that day: and not to me only, but unto all them also that love his appearing."

The crown is not only personal to him, but universal, only limited " unto all them that love his appearing." Here it is not simply love for Jesus personally, but love for the great fact which is to culminate in the great glory of Jesus. To "love his appearing" there is the absolute necessity for loving His Person. The loving His coming is the test of loving His Person. We love the fact because we love the Person. We are not charged to love any theory or opinion about the manner of His coming, or the time, but the fact. Let Him come when He will, how He will, and for what purpose He will. We love His coming because we love Him. "Even so, come quickly, Lord Jesus," and bring Thy heaven with Thee.

The overcomers, the victorious ones, the conquerors, they are the heaven-crowned ones. Their valorous strength, their undaunted courage, their dire conflicts, their unyielding steadfastness, their holding fast even unto death; they who, by their Christian constancy and courage, keep themselves unharmed and spotless from all the devices, assaults, solicitations of the world, the flesh and the devil—these are crowned to the heavenly life.

They have gained the victory over the devil; conquerors they are of him. "I write unto you young men because ye have overcome the wicked one." The spirit of antichrist they have overcome. "For whatsoever is born of God overcometh the world; and this is the victory that overcometh the world, even our faith. Who is he that overcometh the world but he that believeth that Jesus is the Son of God." "He that overcometh shall inherit all things; and I will be his God, and he shall be my son." Blessed company! "They all are robed in spotless white. And conquering palms they bear." They are the victors. The conflict is past, the battle has been fought, and the victory has been won and won forever. They are "more than conquerors through him that loved them." The blessed Jesus has always led them in triumph, and now they are with Him upon His throne in their last and great triumph.

This love is born of the Spirit of God and is centered on Jesus Christ. Heaven depends on our love to the Saviour of sinners. We love heaven only as we love Him and as we seek for Him. This love is to be ardent and supreme. Jesus is the joy and glory of heaven.

> Do not I love thee, O my Lord?
>   Then let me nothing love;
> Dead be my heart to every joy,
>   When Jesus cannot move.
>
> Thou know'st I love thee, dearest Lord,
>   But O, I long to soar
> Far from the sphere of mortal joys,
>   And learn to love thee more!

X

LOOKING TO HEAVEN

"Salvation, salvation is the only necessary thing. This clay-idol, the world, is not to be sought; it is a morsel not for you, but for hunger-bitten bastards. Contend for salvation. Your master, Christ, won heaven with strokes. It is a besieged castle, it must be taken with violence. Oh, this world thinketh heaven but at the next door, and that godliness may sleep in a bed of down, till it come to heaven! But that will not do it."

—SAMUEL RUTHERFORD.

THE Christian's attitude to heaven is one of desire. Paul puts it thus: "I am in a strait betwixt two, having the desire to depart and be with Christ, which is far better." To set one's heart upon, longing for heaven, a great desire for Jesus, to be with Him—that was Paul's attitude. The very best Jesus has is for His disciples. God gives Jesus the key to everything, and Jesus turns everything over to His followers. This ought to kindle and inflame desire. We ought not, we cannot move heavenward with a chilled heart, a cold purpose, a frigid resolution. "For in this we groan, earnestly desiring to be clothed upon with our house which is from heaven: If so be that being clothed we shall not be found naked."

It is, it must be, an *earnest desire*. We start to heaven in a flame and it ought to be fanned to an intense flame at each step.

The Christian's attitude is toward heaven, not to die, merely to be unclothed of the present. It is not simply to get rid of the cumbrance of the tent-like bodies. It is not death, for death has no charms for the true Christian. He fears not to die, he fears not to live. Life has for him little charms apart from heaven. Death has no charms aside from heaven.

The attitude is thus given by Paul: "For we that are in this tabernacle do groan, being burdened; not for that we would be unclothed, but clothed upon, that mortality might be swallowed up of life." This supposes a desire so full of light, of expectations, of longings, that it burdens. Heaven is so charmful to the unclouded vision of faith, so bright and deathless under the rosy hues of an immortal hope, that the present burdens become an intolerable load. To stay is to live in the graveyard, to have a home in a decaying house, to be dying. Earth is a vast cemetery. Everything betokens death, breathes death and is dying. The desire of heaven is kindled at the fountain of life where we become sick of the dead and sick of the dying. The soul, having tasted of the spring of life, longs to bathe in its full river, and yearns to plunge in its immeasurable ocean.

The attitude for heaven is the desire of life for

life, of life against death. Here death reigns, imprisons and ruins. There life reigns, emancipates and enriches. We are impatiently patient for life eternal, life which is found nowhere else but in heaven. Sick of death, we aspire to life by living and longing for heaven. This groaning for heaven is not natural. Nature is of the earth, earthly. The Holy Spirit changes nature and fashions us for heaven. "Now he that hath wrought us for the selfsame thing is God, who also hath given us the earnest of the Spirit."

God has fashioned us for this heavenly life. He implants in us these heavenly desires. When we stand thus attested to heaven, thus looking toward heaven, thus longing for heaven, these are the marks of God's hand, the results of His work of grace in our hearts. He puts in us the Holy Spirit to keep the memory freighted with and alive to the fact of heaven, to keep the desires ardent for heaven, to keep the hands busy for heaven and to keep the taste sweet and fresh for heaven. God works this mighty heavenly work in us so that we look not at the things which are temporal, value not the things which are insipid and transitory, and strive not after the perishing things of earth.

These are materialized and materializing times. Materialized times always make much of earth and little of heaven. True religion always makes little of earth and much of heaven. If God's watchmen are not brave, argus-eyed, and sleepless, religion will catch the contagion of the times, and think little of and struggle less for heaven.

God makes much of heaven. He was the architect and builder of its magnificence and glory. It is His dwelling place, His city, by preëminence, His capital, His metropolis, the home of His family, the dwelling place of His earthly elect. God fashions every child of His after the pattern of heaven, feeds every child of His on its food, trains every soldier of His for its warfare, and begets in every child of His insatiable thirstings for heaven. When the taste is dull heavenward and the eye dim heavenward, then the luster of God has faded from the spirit, the work of God is checked in the soul, the life of God pulsates feebly, and the love of God is chilled to the heart.

"For this selfsame thing"—this heavenly fashion, these heavenly tastes and heavenly longings—says the apostle, "has God wrought in us and given us the earnest of his Spirit." Not only does this work of God wrought in us shape and mold us after the heavenly, but the true work of God in us gives a foretaste and pledge of the heavenly.

To the true Christian, heaven is not a mere sentiment, or poetry, or dreamland, but real solid and abiding granite in strength, home-drawing in sweetness and influence. God is never happier, never better to His earthly saints than when their

heavenly trend is strongly marked. Heavenly longings and heavenly goings are plainly and emphatically declared of the saints whose devotion to
heaven has unloosed and estranged them from
earth. He is not ashamed to be called their God.
For them He hath prepared a city. What does
God think of us who have no sighings for heaven,
no longings for it; earth, earthly, earthened?
God's throne is in heaven. His power, person and
glory are preëminently there. Does God attract
and hold us? Then heaven attracts and holds. Do
we thirst after God?

> Jerusalem, my happy home!
>   Name ever dear to me!
> When shall my labors have an end,
>   In joy and peace, and thee?
>
> When shall these eyes thy heaven-built walls
>   And pearly gates behold?
> Thy bulwarks with salvation strong,
>   And streets of shining gold?
>
> O when, thou city of my God,
>   Shall I thy courts ascend,
> Where congregations ne'er break up,
>   And sabbaths have no end?

XI

ON A STRETCH FOR HEAVEN

"God will manage our affairs if we are filled with His affairs. Be sure you are in God's hands and not that of an ecclesiasticism. I am very feeble. I want to live for God and to depart and be with Christ. I have an unspeakable desire to know the future, to see it and enjoy it, and to be there to see and enjoy. Let us hold on to God."

—E. M. BOUNDS.

ON a stretch for heaven is the Christian's attitude, with all his power taxed and strained in a movement, a conflict, a race for heaven. "Know ye not that they which run in a race, run all, but one receiveth the prize? So run that ye may obtain. And every man that striveth for the mastery is temperate in all things. Now they do it to obtain a corruptible crown; but we an incorruptible. I therefore so run, not as uncertainly; so fight I, not as one that beateth the air: But I keep under my body, and bring it into subjection: lest that by any means, when I have preached to others, I myself should be a castaway."

Here we have the picture of the heavenly athlete putting forth all his trained strength to win the prize of an incorruptible crown. The Greek athlete, in his exhaustive exertion to win the corruptible crown, is a favorite Bible illustration as a

stimulant to stir men for heaven. The athlete has
no eye but for the crown. Every part and particle
of his strength is put under strain to secure that
end, and we are charged to " so run that we may
obtain."

Jesus impresses the same idea on the multitude
in reply to the inquiry: " Then said one unto him,
Lord, are there few that be saved? And he said
unto them, Strive to enter in at the straight gate;
for many, I say unto you, will seek to enter in, and
shall not be able." *Strive* means *to agonize*. It is
the word for intensity of effort, and effort that includes the outlay of the fullest strength in an earnest and impassioned way.

In Hebrews, twelfth chapter, we have a most
vivid picturesque declaration of the same great
truth that heaven is gained only by the most intense and persistent effort, which taxes all the
strength and demands the outlay of all possible
energy to secure it. The old worthies are represented as having gained the prize, and ranged themselves as spectators of the renowned and exciting
conflict, and Jesus Christ is set forth as having
passed over and marked the way and seated Himself at the goal to adjudge the race, and award the
crown. The racers are charged most solemnly,
" Wherefore, seeing we also are compassed about
with so great a cloud of witnesses, let us lay aside
every weight, and the sin which doth so easily be-
set us, and let us run with patience the race that is

set before us; looking unto Jesus, the author and finisher of our faith; who for the joy that was set before him, endured the cross, despising the shame, and is set down at the right hand of the throne of God."

Where in all the pages of literature and appeals could there be a stronger call to throw all energy and all weight into the conflict? The issue trembles on the racer, his ability to run, to outstrip and to lay aside all things which embarrass, or impede progress. Heaven is staked on the issue. An incorruptible crown is the reward of successful running. Immortality and eternal life hang on the issue.

Paul charges Timothy to be on the same stretch for heaven. The people will not be on the stretch for heaven if their preachers are not so. Paul desires Timothy to lay himself out in the race, to "fight the good fight of faith." The word "fight" is one of intense effort—agonize the good agony. Paul had been writing to Timothy about the wish to be rich, the love of money and its pernicious and damning results. Then he charges him to flee as a man of God from these things, and as worldly men agonize with desire and toil after money, and so eagerly pursue after it in order to lay hold on earthly riches, so as a man of God he was to put out agonizing and continuous effort, not for earth and its money, but for heaven and its inestimable and imperishable riches.

In the Epistle to the Philippians, we have a vivid view of Paul on a stretch for heaven:

"That I may know him, and the power of his resurrection, and the fellowship of his sufferings, being made conformable unto his death; if by any means I might attain unto the resurrection of the dead. Not as though I had already attained, either were already perfect; but I follow after, if that I may apprehend that for which also I am apprehended of Christ Jesus. Brethren, I count not myself to have apprehended; but this one thing I do, forgetting those things which are behind, and reaching forth unto those things which are before, I press toward the mark for the prize of the high calling of God in Christ Jesus. Let us, therefore, as many as be perfect, be thus minded; and if in anything ye be otherwise minded, God shall reveal even this unto you."

Paul purposed to win heaven, not by his marvelous conversion, nor by his high apostolate, but by laying himself out for heaven all his life. On a stretch for heaven Paul was, with all the energy of his imperial nature and with all the ardor and intensity he could command, "forgetting those things which are behind," in the eagerness and strength of his forward pressing. "Reaching forth to those that are before," means stretching one's self forward in eagerness, energy and intentiveness of pursuit. "I press toward the mark" is the figure of running with swiftness and an energy which is continued. All this indicates the most engaging and absorbing interest and effort, and shows a perseverance with all the forces stretched to their utmost tension, in order to hold the whole being to the farthest and fullest outlay of strength to gain the end.

Paul, the great apostle, was on the full stretch for heaven. He could not afford to miss heaven. " I therefore so run, not as uncertainly; so fight I, not as one that beateth the air: But I keep under my body, and bring it into subjection: lest that by any means, when I have preached to others, I myself should be a castaway." Thus does he express his feelings and purpose. An apostle, the chief one though he be, can only make sure of heaven by being on the stretch after it always and everywhere. May this example stir us to the profoundest depths. " Brethren, be followers together of me, and mark them which walk so as ye have us for an ensample."

> Racers of Christ, arise,
>   Stand forth, prepare to run:
> Toward the goal lift up your eyes,
>   And manfully go on.
>
> 'Tis true the race is short,
>   But then it is not long;
> Each racer soon will take his harp,
>   And warble Zion's song.

XII

KNOWLEDGE OF HEAVEN

"Fasten your grips fast on Christ. Let not 'this clay portion of earth take up your soul. It is the portion of bastards, and ye are a child of God. Therefore, seek your Father's heritage. Send up your heart to see the dwelling house and fair rooms in the New City. Fy, fy, upon those who cry, 'Up with the world, and down with conscience and heaven!'"

—Samuel Rutherford.

THE Christian's attitude to heaven is one of *knowledge*.

"For we know that, if our earthly house of this tabernacle were dissolved, we have a building of God, a house not made with hands, eternal in the heavens" (2 Cor. 5:1).

The Christian stands in regard to the certainty of death as all the living do. A frail fleeting Arab tent is his body, the heir of death and hastening to decay. But the Christian knows that "if this earthly house were dissolved, he has a house not made with hands eternal in the heavens."

It is real knowledge about heaven, not a mere wish, or hope so, or a happy guess, but assured

115

knowledge, a fact communicated, knowledge imparted. God has committed Himself in the strongest way to give knowledge and assurance of heaven to every child of God. "The Spirit himself bears witness" to our adoption and heirship. In regard to this great fact of our names being written in the Book of Life, we are not left in ignorance. God seals us with the Holy Spirit which is the earnest as well as a witness. A witness bears testimony. The earnest is both the pledge of heaven and its foretaste. Heaven he has in conscious realization, not in full measure, but in a measure realized. The true Christian is no agnostic. He knows some things.

Heaven in this life is not to him as large a reality, but as much a reality as it will be when his feet are on the gold pavement of the heavenly city. Heaven pervades and sweetens his whole life. His faith brings to him the very substance of things hoped for, and his hope makes the present luminous by its light and strong by its strength. Christian faith and hope make the things of heaven real, conscious, tangible, experimented. How the knowledge of his home in heaven defies death, change, and misfortune! How attractive that knowledge makes it! A "building of God, eternal in the heavens!"

Human hands poison with decay our fairest earthly homes. The touch of human hands has defiled them. Death awaits them. Our palace across the river draws us without regret, but with delight, away from our earthly tent, our clay hut. He has had but little of God, and none of the sweets of faith, who has not anticipated in the earthly the reality and joy of the heavenly. Are we to be tossed in uncertainty as to our home on high? Is there no blessed surety? Yes, we know. The Word of God tells us so. The Spirit of God has spoken it to our hearts, and left its sweetness and its picture there. We have been examining our title deeds lately. They are heavenly deeds, signed and sealed. The house is built, the lot is numbered, all named in our bond, and " we *know* that if our earthly house of this tabernacle were dissolved, we have a building of God, a house not made with hands, eternal in the heavens." Death makes no bankrupt of the Christian. It only brings him to his inheritance. Death is the best thing that can come to the Christian. It puts him in possession of his great fortune. It brings him to his home. We ought never to sigh; we should go through with radiance and triumph. We ought always and everywhere, like the saints of old, " to take joyfully the spoiling of our possessions, knowing in ourselves that in heaven we have a better and enduring substance."

> Thine earthly Sabbaths, Lord, we love;
> But there's a nobler rest above:
> To that our lab'ring souls aspire,
> With ardent pangs of strong desire.

No more fatigue, no more distress;
Nor sin nor hell shall reach the place;
No sighs shall mingle with the songs
Which warble from immortal tongues.

No rude alarms of raging foes;
No cares to break the long repose;
No midnight shade, no clouded sun,
But sacred, high, eternal noon.

O long-expected day, begin;
Dawn on these realms of woe and sin:
Fain would we leave this weary road,
And sleep in death, to rest with God.

XIII

CITIZENSHIP OF HEAVEN

"Love heaven. Let your heart be in it. Up, up and visit the new land and view the fair city, and the white throne and the Lamb—run fast for it is late."

—SAMUEL RUTHERFORD.

THE Bible puts our citizenship in heaven by such a naturalization force, that we are expatriated from earth, and have always the sighings of an exile for native land, and the weariness, longings and loneliness of pilgrims and strangers. The Bible puts all true Christians in the attitude of groaning after heaven, on a stretch for living for heaven. To them it is the only life, life indeed—to live for heaven, and to live in heaven.

The term heaven signifies a place of exaltation and glory. It is God's dwelling place. The immediate presence of God is there. It is the land of a higher order of beings and a higher order of things than exist on earth.

It is called " the third heaven " from its loftiness and supremacy, in contrast with the lower heavens. This term has been fully accepted in modern piety as the designation of the place. The good man is to lay up his treasures in heaven, on which his heart and eye are to be constantly fixed. Heaven is the place to which Jesus has gone, where He is preparing a place for us. Heaven is a place, a land very dear to the Christian's heart. Heaven! how the heart beats quicker and the eye grows brighter at the mention of it! The eye of faith holds it in vision, and to it the prayer of faith is lifted. " Our Father " dwells there. Jesus came from heaven on His great mission. The Holy Spirit came down from heaven. The bodies of Enoch and Elijah and of Christ are there. Perhaps the bodies of the saints who came out of their graves when Jesus was raised from the dead are in heaven. The spirits of all the holy dead are there. A holy place is heaven, a happy place it is. An innumerable company are there, safe, blessed, tearless, and immortal.

How heaven ought to draw on our hearts and lift us above earth! How it should fill our thoughts and brighten our hopes! Heaven ought to assuage our griefs, banish our fears, lift care from our hearts and make us immune to the ills of this life. Jesus was ever lifting His eye and heart to heaven, ever speaking and thinking of His Father in heaven, ever looking at heaven, that, supported by its sight and joy, He might " endure the cross and despise the shame." He made much of heaven. So also ought we to make much of heaven. It ought to be the land in which we live, its atmosphere should surround us, its glories allure us and its deathless beauties fill eye and heart. It should be the aim of our lives, the goal of our ambition, the stimulant of every exertion. Our names should be written there, our treasures laid up there.

Heaven in symbol is native land, fatherland, home.

" For our conversation is in heaven; from whence also we look for the Saviour, the Lord Jesus Christ " (Phil. 3:20).

The word, " conversation," the Revised Version changes to " citizenship," and in the margin it has " commonwealth." The word has to do with a state, a commonwealth, its laws, regulations and citizens.

" To-day," said Jesus to the dying thief, " shalt thou be with me in paradise." Paul said he " was caught up into paradise," the paradise of God, a place enclosed and beautiful, like the abode of our first parents, another name for Eden. The name is transferred to the abode of the saints in heaven, which is called the " Paradise of God." The first paradise was made for man, with every tree that is pleasant to the sight and good for food. Beauty and purity and innocence were there. These all will be in the second paradise in larger proportion. The first paradise: " The Lord God planted a garden." The second paradise: " God hath prepared for them a city." The contrast and advance are from a garden to a city. The first was *man's paradise*. The second, the "paradise of God." Man was in the first paradise. God is in the second paradise. God *visited* the first paradise. He *dwells* in the second paradise!

It involves the common well-being and happiness of the whole people, and not of any favored caste or class. The perfection of government is heaven, in which the well-being and happiness of each and all are secured and enjoyed to the fullest measure.

In the last part of the above quotation, we have the idea of heaven as a place brought strongly out, "heaven, from whence also we look for the Saviour." Jesus with His human body must occupy a place, so represented constantly in the New Testament, and that place, heaven, and from that place, heaven, we look for Him to come and do His work of raising the dead and changing the bodies of His saints.

"Who shall change our vile body, that it may be fashioned like unto his glorious body, according to the working whereby he is able even to subdue all things unto himself" (Phil. 3:21).

The Christian has his citizenship in heaven. His allegiance is to God, his loyalty to heaven. The laws of heaven he is bound to obey. The best citizen of heaven is the best citizen of earth. He is bound by highest obligations to obedience, to virtue, to government. How it exalts to be a citizen of such a divine commonwealth! "I am a Roman," carried with it in the days of Rome's power, dignity and honor, safety and sacredness. "I am a citizen of heaven." What dignity and nobility, purity and heavenliness, such citizenship ought to represent!

> O Paradise! O Paradise!
>   I want to sin no more,
> I want to be as pure on earth
>   As on thy spotless shore;
>
> O Paradise! O Paradise!
>   I greatly long to see
> The special place my dearest Lord
>   In love prepares for me;
>
> Lord Jesus, King of Paradise,
>   O keep me in thy love,
> And guide me to that happy land
>   Of perfect rest above.

XIV

HEAVEN A HOME

"Heaven is called a kingdom for its immense greatness, and a city because of its great beauty and population. It is full of inhabitants of all nations, where are many angels, and an infinite number of the just, even as many as have died since the death of Abel. And thither shall repair all such as shall die in Christ to the end of the world; and after the general judgment shall there remain forever invested in their glorious bodies. How happy will it be to live with such persons."

—JEREMY TAYLOR.

THE Epistle to the Hebrews, eleventh chapter, speaking of Old Testament Saints says:

" These all died in faith, not having received the promises, but having seen them afar off, and were persuaded of them, and embraced them, and confessed that they were strangers and pilgrims on the earth. For they that say such things declare plainly that they seek a country." The Revised Version changes this so that it reads: " For they that say such things make it manifest that they are seeking after a country of their own." Dean Alford, in his Commentary, translates it thus, " That they seek after a home." The English word

" country," does not give the idea strong enough. The word is defined, one's native country, one's fatherland, one's own country. Heaven is our home, our fatherland. Here we are foreigners, pilgrims and strangers. The heart of a stranger, the loneliness and longing of a stranger, the efforts and weariness of the pilgrims, should be ours. The heart-sighing, the exiled yearnings, should declare to all plainly that we are not at home, that we are not native to these skies, but heaven-born, seeking the heavenly country.

Heaven ought to draw and engage us. Heaven ought to so fill our hearts and hands, our manner and our conversation, our character and our features, that all would see that we are foreigners, strangers to this world, natives of a nobler clime, fairer than this. Out of tune, out of harmony, out of course, we must be with this world. The very atmosphere of the world should be chilling to us and noxious, its suns eclipsed and its companionship dull and insipid. Heaven is our native land and home to us, and death to us is not the dying hour, but the birth hour. Heaven should kindle desire, and like a magnet draw us upward to the skies. Duty, inexorable duty, fealty to God, alone, should hold us here.

A beautiful, gifted young woman once said that she had not seen one minute for several years wherein she desired to live one moment longer for the sake of any other good in life but doing good, living to God and doing what might be to His glory.

Paul was brought into a strait between desire and duty. Christ and heaven had his heart, but duty kept him in exile. " For me to live is Christ but to die is gain. But if I live in the flesh this is the fruit of my labor: yet what I shall choose I wot not. For I am in a strait betwixt two, having a desire to depart and be with Christ which is far better. Nevertheless to abide in the flesh is more needful for you. And having this confidence, I know that I shall abide and continue with you all for your furtherance and joy of faith." With Paul it was as it ever should be. Duty retires desire, and teaches it to wait till the glad hour of its fruition.

Of those ancient believers spoken of in Hebrews 11, we discover that they all were pilgrims and strangers on the earth with heavenly longings and heavenly seeking. Alas, for the hearts which are settled here! Heaven to them is a strange, an alien, a far-off land! A background these had. They had left the earthland and refused to go back to it. They had transferred their home and their home-land to the better and heavenly country. God noted their fidelity, heard their sighing, and noted seeking. He was not ashamed of them and built for them a city. It is God-built. That assures its location, its glory, its eternity, and its bliss.

In writing to the Corinthians of the Christian

attitude to heaven, Paul says, as we have it in the Revised Version, "We are willing rather to be absent from the body and to be at home with the Lord." Here we have one of the strongest, sweetest, most attractive symbols of heaven. Whatever there is in that place we call home—sacred, dear, restful, delightful, full of holy feelings and deathless ties, all these are predicted in a form ten thousand fold stronger and sweeter of heaven.

At home in heaven! What welcome! What satisfaction! What rest to tired feet, and tired hearts! What a sense of security and confidence! The home feelings in full opulence of richest wealth! Nowhere on earth's green, glad soil will the home feeling be so profound, so satisfying, so restful, and so happifying as in heaven. It is not only to be realized as home when we get there, but all along the way the home feeling is to draw and bind us to that heavenly world. The homesickness for heaven is to alienate us from earth, make us sick at heart and beget pinings for home.

With deep spiritual insight and the soundest spiritual philosophy did one of Scotland's most gifted and saintly preachers say after visiting a beautiful Manse: " The Manse is altogether too sweet. Other men could hardly live there without saying, this is my rest. I don't think ministers' manses should ever be so beautiful."

This is not splenetic, nor overdrawn, but the assertion of a great principle to guard against a great peril. Great earthly attachments lessen heavenly attachments. The heart which indulges itself in great earthly loves will have less for heaven. God's great work and often His most afflictive and chastening work is to unfasten our hearts from earth and fasten them to heaven, to break up and desolate the earthly home that we may seek a home in heaven.

My heavenly home is bright and fair:
Nor pain nor death can enter there;
Its glittering towers the sun outshine;
That heavenly mansion shall be mine.

Let others seek a home below,
Which flames devour, or waves o'erflow,
Be mine the happier lot to own
A heavenly mansion near the throne.
—*William Hunter.*

XV

TRIBULATION AND HEAVEN

"There is required patience on our part till the summer fruit of heaven be ripe for us. It is in the bud; but there be many things to do before our harvest come. And we take ill with it, and can hardly endure to set our paper-face to one of Christ's storms, and to go to heaven with wet feet. . . . We love to carry a heaven to heaven with us, and would have two summers in one year, and no less than two heavens. But this will not do for us; one (and such a one!) may suffice us well enough. Christ got but one only, and shall we have two?"

—Samuel Rutherford.

THE odium and persecution cast upon followers of God, goes like a knife to many a saintly heart and makes them "men of sorrows and acquainted with grief." They are shut out. Religion of the most heavenly type is cast out by religion. No persecutors are so heartless and relentless as religious persecutors. No hatred is so bitter as the world's hatred. "If the world hate you, ye know that it hated me before it hated you. If ye were of the world, the world would love his own; but because ye are not of the world, but I have chosen you out of the world, therefore the world hateth you. Remember the word that I said unto you, The servant is not greater than his lord. If they have persecuted me, they will also persecute you."

But wherever these persecutions come from, and from whom they come, they become the means of purity and maturity. By them God's people are purged and perfected. We are not to repine at them, nor be impatient under them! We are not to fight against them, nor murmur at them, but endure them, endure with sweetness and joy; says James: " My brethren, count it all joy when ye fall into divers temptations; knowing this, that the trying of your faith worketh patience. But let patience have her perfect work, that ye may be perfect and entire, wanting nothing." This is the process.

Paul brings to our minds the same view of trials. Putting Jesus Christ to the forefront, and our relation to Him of justification and its rapturous peace as the result of faith, that faith giving us fuller access to Him and a farther vision and a higher and firmer standing. It brings heaven into full view, with the presence of Christ and the glory of God shining through the door of unclouded, undying hope!

"And not only so, but we glory in tribulations also, knowing that tribulation worketh patience; And patience, experience; and experience, hope" (Rom. 5:3).

Every holy principle, every precious result, every fragrant sentiment, brought to us by faith in Jesus, is enlarged by tribulation. By it patience is made more patient, enriched in sweetness and in strength, and experience more firmly fixed, deeper rooted, made steadfast and immovable. Hope is enlarged in scope and vision, increased in luster, and its foundations are laid in jeweled adornment. "We glory in tribulations." Do we? Can we? Heaven in eye and heart enables us to do this strange work, for tribulations not only burnish and garnish our heavenly home, but add many rooms to its size and many gems to its beauty and value.

Peter leaves his normal, prosy, thankless service of "stirring up pure minds by way of remembrance," and rises to vision, beatitude and anthem:

"Blessed be the God and Father of our Lord Jesus Christ, which according to his abundant mercy hath begotten us again unto a lively hope by the resurrection of Jesus Christ from the dead. To an inheritance incorruptible, and undefiled, and that fadeth not away, reserved in heaven for you, who are kept by the power of God through faith unto salvation, ready to be revealed in the last time. Wherein ye greatly rejoice, though now for a season, if need be, ye are in heaviness through manifold temptations: That the trial of your faith, being much more precious than of gold that perisheth, though it be tried with fire, might be found unto praise and honor and glory at the appearing of Jesus Christ.

Whom having not seen ye love: in whom, though now ye see him not, yet believing, ye rejoice with joy unspeakable and full of glory " (1 Peter 1:3).

Here they all are—God the Father, Jesus and His resurrection, the Spirit and sanctification, hope, heaven, love and fiery trials. The trials clarify, refine, aid the beatific outburst, and swell the anthems unto praise and honor and glory. Trials have brought heaven into a clearer and nearer vision, perfected the faith, purified the love, and swelled the joy, till it becomes unspeakable and full of glory.

" Counting it all joy " is not simply resignation. That as a cardinal virtue and crowning grace, is scarcely recognized as a grace at all in times of robust faith. It is not the grace of folded arms and silent hearts, but it is " Count it all joy." It is, " Glory in tribulations also." Glory in tribulations like you glory in heaven, for they are one and inseparable. Rejoice greatly! Rejoice with " joy unspeakable and full of glory." Rejoice in the prospect of heaven.

Glory in infirmities. Says Paul: " Therefore, I take pleasure in infirmities, in reproaches, in necessities, in persecutions, in distresses for Christ's sake; for when I am weak, then am I strong."

The beatitudes are born here, and enlarged to their largest measure and most heavenly joy. " Blessed are they which are persecuted for righteousness' sake, for theirs is the kingdom of heaven.

Blessed are ye, when men shall revile you, and persecute you, and shall say all manner of evil against
you falsely, for my sake. Rejoice, and be exceeding glad: for great is your reward in heaven; for
so persecuted they the prophets which were before
you." So says Christ, and He puts it among His
diamond utterances, itself a diamond of the first
water. Listen to Paul again:

"For which cause we faint not; but though our
outward man perish, yet the inward man is renewed
day by day. For our light affliction, which is but for
a moment, worketh for us a far more exceeding and
eternal weight of glory; while we look not at the
things which are seen, but at the things which are
not seen. For the things which are seen are temporal, but the things which are not seen are eternal"
(2 Cor. 16–18).

How Paul discredits and eases the pang of every
pain and persecution! "Light affliction"—light
in weight and short in time. It is light compared
with "the weight of glory." It is short compared
with the "eternal weight of glory." Highly prized
and invaluable are these afflictions as they "work
for us a far more exceeding and eternal weight of
glory." Add this estimate to Christ's words,
"Rejoice and be exceeding glad, for great is your
reward in heaven."

But these trials work this exceeding and eternal
greatness of reward only while "we look not at

the things which are seen but at the things which are unseen." The eyes are off of earth—eyes are on heaven. Eyes are off of the things of earth— eyes on the things of heaven.

The reward is sure. The " far more exceeding and eternal weight of glory " is ours. When eyes are on the earth, the things of earth fret and wear the trials into our heart's core, and cause us to lose heaven and all the measureless and imperishable good which these trials bring.

Paul takes the sum, and calculates and judges between the suffering of this life and the glory of the future life: " For I reckon that the sufferings of this present time are not worthy to be compared with the glory which shall be revealed in us." The saints of old had such an estimate of heavenly things and such a low estimate of earthly things, that poverty enhanced heavenly riches: " They took joyfully the spoiling of their goods, knowing in themselves that they had in heaven a better and enduring substance."

Peter couples the two thoughts, suffering and heaven, and asserts that it is a common principle to which they are not to be strangers: " Beloved, think it not strange concerning the fiery trial which is to try you, as though some strange thing hap- pened unto you. But rejoice, inasmuch as ye are partakers of Christ's sufferings; that, when his glory shall be revealed, ye may be glad also with exceeding joy. If ye be reproached for the name of Christ, happy are ye; for the Spirit of glory and of God resteth upon you: on their part, he is evil spoken of, but on your part he is glorified."

Again Peter, when speaking of the devil, he declares the universality of affliction wherever saints are found: "Be sober, be vigilant; because your adversary, the devil, as a roaring lion, walketh about, seeking whom he may devour; whom resist steadfast in the faith, knowing that the same afflictions are accomplished in your brethren that are in the world. But the God of grace, who hath called us unto his eternal glory by Christ Jesus, after that ye have suffered a while, make you perfect, establish, strengthen, settle you."

Heaven is declared to be God's eternal glory. These are words far beyond the dictionaries of earth. The glory of earth's greatest one, though a fading glory, would be much honor, enough to stir the mightiest ambition and gratify the loftiest aspiration. But God's eternal glory! What measure is equal to it? What words can define? What ambition compass? And yet to that we are called, to God's glory! To God's " eternal glory," awake ambition worthy of God! Awake hope as limitless as eternity and as endless! It is not to be revealed till we have suffered a while! Oh, happy suffering! Oh, short suffering, indefinable in its shortness and limited in its pain, when contrasted with God's eternal glory, of which trials are the glory and the usher.

This chastening process often comes through persecutions from the hands of evil men and devils, and yet God holds the control and results of the process in His own hands. Nothing is outside of His power, nothing excluded from His control for the good of His children. "All things," whether they be things from the devil or bad men, or the mistakes of good men; "we know that all things work together for good to them that love God, to them who are the called according to his purpose." Nothing of the nature of persecution and affliction can hinder God from pressing His faithful elect ones on till they are glorified.

"They that will live godly in Christ Jesus shall suffer persecution." "In the world ye shall have tribulation." "If we be dead with him, we shall also live with him. If we suffer, we shall also reign with him." These are axiomatic in the Christ life. There is no persecuting Romish power now, either pagan or papal. Those fierce and cruel days are gone, perhaps forever, but there are petty persecutions. The world still hates Christ's saints, and a worldly church still ostracizes and bans God's peculiar people.

Dr. Adoniram Judson writes from Burmah to a friend in America: " Remember, I pray you, that word of Brainerd. Do not think it enough to live at the rate of common Christians. True, they will call you uncharitable and censorious, but what is the opinion of poor worms of the dust that it should deter us from our duty? Remember that other word of the same holy man, ' Time is but a moment, life a vapor, and all its enjoyments but empty bubbles and fleeting blasts of wind.' " Again Dr. Judson writes, " Let me beg of you not to rest contented with the commonplace religion that is now prevalent."

Yet it is this rising above the commonplace, current religion that gives offense, that awakens opposition, and kindles the fires of a petty, yet painful persecution. No person does much for God, no person seeks heaven in a real, honest, successful way, who does not rise above the average piety.

The Apostle Paul charges Timothy to " follow after righteousness, godliness, faith, love, patience, meekness. Fight the good fight of faith, lay hold of eternal life," giving the most vital relation between the " following after " these things and the " laying hold of eternal life." Heaven is won by winning the heavenly virtues. Ardent pursuit after the graces which constitute heaven is the only way to pursue heaven with ardor and gain the prize. To mature and perfect these graces is to be made ready for heaven.

Patience is one of those fundamental Christian virtues in which we are schooled for the heavenly life. Paul, writing to Romans, says: " To them who by patient continuance in well doing, seek for glory and honor and immortality, eternal life." Again he says: " In your patience ye shall win your souls," as the Revised Version reads.   Patience is defined as the grace of holding out, endurance, literally staying, remaining behind, steadfastness. He is patient who is unswerved from his deliberate purpose and his loyalty to faith and piety by even the greatest trials and sufferings.   Patience is a cardinal virtue in Christian character.   Its importance cannot be overrated.   It is strong and sweet, the pillar of strength, the adornment of beauty.   It does not succumb under suffering.   It is self-restrained.   It does not retaliate wrongs.   Brave it is, opposed to cowardice or despondency, and has nothing in common with wrath and revenge, a gentle grace of serenity and sweetness.   It expresses its sweetness through every bruised and bleeding pore.   It goes to make up a summary of the gospel power and grace.   It is " the kingdom and patience of our Lord Jesus Christ."

Patience is born and perfected in trial.   " We glory," says Paul, " in tribulation also, knowing that tribulation worketh patience."   In James we have this remarkable demand and statement: " Count it all joy when ye fall into divers temptations, knowing this that the trial of your faith worketh patience.   But let patience have her perfect work that ye may be perfect and entire, wanting nothing."   Count every trial joy, not resignation simply, but joy, gladness.   All joy, no part distressful or sad.   Joy at their coming, joy at their results.   This is the way perfection comes.   " Per-

fect and entire, wanting nothing," every grace
present, every grace mature.   Trials bring perfection, maturity, fulness.   God makes our fruit perfect by perfecting our character, and character is
perfected by trial.

How necessary this patience is to the winning
heaven we are not left in doubt.   " For ye have
need of patience, that, after ye have done the will
of God, ye might receive the promises."   " Let us
run with patience the race that is set before us."
Job is the illustration of patience because he held
on to God without variance or shadow of turning
through his manifold trials.   " The Lord gave and
the Lord hath taken away.   Blessed be the name
of the Lord," is the language of patience in its un-
disturbed, uncomplaining serenity and sweetness.
" Though He slay me yet will I trust in Him," is
the language of patience in its endurance and perseverance.

Impatience is the epidemic sin.   Strong people
are impatient, weak people are impatient, sick people are impatient, well people are impatient, old
people are impatient, young people are impatient.
All people try our patience.   So how appropriate
the trying, difficult, universal injunction, " Be patient toward all men "!   Patience is necessary to
fruit bearing.   They who are ready to be reaped
for the heavenly harvest, " keep the word and
bring forth fruit with patience."   This grace seems
to be slow, indolent and always waiting.   Not so,

Christian patience is very quiet, often silent, but never lazy, "not slothful, but followers of them who through faith and patience inherit the promises." Heaven is for the patient spirit. Heaven is already possessed by the patient. Has patience possessed us?

> Who suffer with our Master here,
> We shall before his face appear
>   And by his side sit down;
> To patient faith the prize is sure,
> And all that to the end endure
>   The cross, shall wear the crown.
>
> Thrice blessèd, bliss-inspiring hope!
> It lifts the fainting spirits up,
>   It brings to life the dead:
> Our conflicts here shall soon be past,
> And you and I ascend at last,
>   Triumphant with our head.
>   —*Charles Wesley.*

XVI

THE HOPE OF HEAVEN

"What was the earthly Paradise in Eden compared to that purchased by the second Adam, who is the Lord from heaven? It is a purchased possession. The price it cost the purchaser every one knows. Having purchased it, He has gone to prepare it, to set it in order, to lay out His skill upon it. O what a place will Jesus make it—yes, has already made heaven. The very place should attract us."
—NEVINS.

IT is not the bare fact of heaven with which we are dealing now, but the Christian grace of heaven, which is hope. There is much delusion in the belief of a mere fact. Such belief is sterile and deludes if the fact is not fashioned into a principle. If the cold facts of Gospel history do not become the fertilizers of the sweet graces of the Spirit, then are they dead and deadening. These facts of the Gospel as they exist in pages of history, even though the pages be inspired, do not save until they enter into our experience and become the bone and blood of our spiritual life. The fact of heaven must be believed. The heaven of fact exists all glorious and enduring, but this fact of heaven must enter our experience, and then of this experience hope is born, the twin in beauty, intelligence and goodness, with faith and love.

Hope is a mighty spiritual principle. So strong is it that the apostle centers all the forces of salvation in it. "We are saved," he says, "by hope." By it there comes into play all the energetic forces which save. These forces are limp and forceless without hope. Heaven nourishes all the principles of a deep, conscious piety. The Christian never works so well, never suffers so well, never grows so well, as when heaven is in full view of his eyes. It is that which gives to hope its ripeness, richness and power. Only the saint who is after heaven with all the ardor and brightness of hope is truly saved. Doubt and fear flee away from such a salvation.

By its characteristics is this heavenly hope distinguished from all false hopes which perish. It is patient. Hope can wait, and lose none of its brightness, wait with serenity and sweetness, wait without murmuring and disquietude. It is "the patience of hope" which adds to its luster and sweetness. "But if we hope for that we see not, then do we with patience wait for it."

It is termed a *good* hope, joined to everlasting consolation. What can be better than a hope which brings in everlasting consolation, a source of perpetual, unfailing joy! It is also termed a "lively" or "living hope." Peter is telling how this true immortal hope came out of the grave of their dead hopes, so vitalized and immortalized by the resurrection of Jesus Christ from the dead, " to an inheritance, incorruptible, undefiled and that fadeth not away." Our hope has the imperishable life of Jesus Christ in it. It is called a blessed hope. Blessed and happy is this hope! It has in it all the beatitudes and all happifying qualities. It makes us happy and ineffable, perennial, sure of happiness.

True Christian hope is only seen by the heart's eye. The Revised Version has it, " The eyes of your heart enlightened that ye may know what is the hope of your calling." Heart eyes and heavenly light in which to see heaven. Our natural eyes and earthly lights do not show us " the calling," neither have they vision for " the riches of the glory of that inheritance " on which hope feeds and lives.

Hope while it flourishes by the afflictions of life, yet is formed of the gentlest and mildest graces. It combines meekness with fear. It is neither arrogant, rude nor self-assertive, but is mild, retiring and reverential. It is a very patient grace. It perseveres, holds on, and is steadfast, strong to wait till its fruition comes, and saves from discontent, depression and weakness.

Hope is one of the three great elements of Christian character. It is found united with faith and love in order to give perfection, to establish Christian reputation, and to awaken thankfulness, because it is so apparent and so robust.

"We give thanks to God always for you all, making mention of you in our prayers; remembering without ceasing, your work of faith, and labor of love, and patience of hope, in our Lord Jesus Christ, in the sight of God and our Father" (1 Thess. 1:2).

While faith exhibits itself in active works love shows itself in exhaustive toil, hope brightens all, and bears all, declaring her sisterhood to the other graces by patient waiting. Hope's bright endurance mightily sustains faith, and love gives to them unfaltering and unfainting courage. They are inseparably united in Christian life.

"And now abideth faith, hope, love, these three; but the greatest of these is love" (1 Cor. 13:13).

"Faith appropriates the grace of God in the facts of salvation. Love is the animating spirit of our Christian life, while hope takes hold of the future as belonging to the Lord, and to those who are His. The kingdom of God, past, present and future is thus reflected in faith, love and hope."

How thoroughly hope impregnates the Gospel system! How essential it is to Christian character! How necessary to Christian struggles will be seen in the many references to it in the New Testament.

" Paul, an apostle of Jesus Christ by the commandment of God our Saviour, and Lord Jesus Christ, which is our hope " (1 Tim. 1:1).

In this passage hope centers itself in our Lord Jesus Christ. He is our hope. We hang on Him, we center all in Him.

This hope of a glorious Christ and a glorious heaven, a glorious and eternal future, is not a product of man's nature, not born of his despair, not the outgrowth of his cheerful spirit, but it is a spiritual gift, a grace in germ and in fruitage.

" Now the God of hope fill you with all joy and peace in believing, that ye may abound in hope, through the power of the Holy Ghost " (Rom. 15: 13).

Hope has its spring and being in God. Founded on faith in God, it floods the soul with joy and peace. It increases by the presence of the Holy Spirit working in us. Hope abounds more and more as we are filled with all the fulness of God. The whole plan of salvation, its mystery and the glory of its riches, are summarized by Paul: " Christ in you the hope of glory." Where Christ is, there this hope springs to its opulent fulness. All is barrenness, death and despair out of Christ.

The hope of heaven is not a mere emotion. It is not fitful, but ever enduring and strong. It burns with a steady, often a brilliant light. It is not an accident, an accompaniment merely, not a mere incident of the religious life, but vital, fundamental, organic. It goes into the being of vital godliness, as an essential principle. It dwells in the Holy of Holies, and is the High Priest of the inner sanctuary of the soul. It sanctifies the Lord God, and dwells where He dwells.

"But sanctify the Lord God in your hearts, and be ready always to give an answer to every man that asketh you a reason of the hope that is in you, with meekness and fear" (1 Peter 3:15).

> In hope of that immortal crown
>   I now the cross sustain,
> And gladly wander up and down,
>   And smile at toil and pain:
> I suffer out my threescore years,
>   Till my Deliverer come,
> And wipe away his servants' tears,
>   And take his exile home.
>   —*Charles Wesley.*

XVIII

REUNION IN HEAVEN

Strike your tent, O pilgrim,
  Gird your loins and follow on;
Soon your journey's ended,
  'Twill bring thee to thy God.'
                    —CLAUD L. CHILTON.

MUCH of deep and positive joy will spring from the reunion of the broken and wasted loves and friendships of earth. We shall see our friends and associate with them in stronger and more hallowed ties, because we had been partners in the tears and toils of earth. The society of heaven stands out conspicuous, and in an intense manner. Its crowds, its multitudes, its city, all express association; and doubtless, while there will be no selfish and exclusive circles, there will be narrow, closer, select ones within the larger. Paul checks our sorrows and modifies our grief for our dead with these words:

"But I would not have you ignorant, brethren, concerning them which are asleep, that ye sorrow not, even as others which have no hope. For if we believe that Jesus died and rose again, even so them also which sleep in Jesus will God bring with him.

For the Lord himself shall descend from heaven with a shout, with the voice of the archangel, and with the trump of God; and the dead in Christ shall rise first. Then we which are alive and remain shall be caught up together with them in the clouds, to meet the Lord in the air; and so shall we ever be with the Lord. Wherefore comfort one another with these words " (1 Thess. 4: 13–18).

What does Paul mean? That we are not to weep in despair over the graves of our loved ones who have left us. Why? Because we have hope. Hope of what? Of meeting them again; and with them, to meet the Lord and be forever with Him, and forever with them. " Wherefore comfort one another with these words." We shall see them again. We shall know them again. We shall be with them forever. These are the points of comfort in the apostle's words. Divine comfort! which even here on earth makes us victors over death, takes his sting away, wipes the tears from our eyes, and wreathes our hearts with fadeless hopes.

Many are the attractions of heaven, all of which should win us from the vain and perishing things of earth. First of all, Jesus, our Great High Priest, is there, the sun and center of that heavenly world. Then the absence of so many things which make earth undesirable—sickness and sorrow, pain and death, with earth's privations, its discomforts, its disappointments. But added to all these glori-

ous things which should draw us as a strong magnet to heaven, is the blessed hope of a glorious reunion with loved ones who left us and have gone
on before.

Not only does Paul give us an intimation of this
pleasing prospect, but John, in Revelation, seventh
chapter, in showing us the things he saw, when " a
door was opened in heaven " to his gaze. He tells
us who are in heaven—God, Jesus Christ, the
Lamb of God, the angels, and those who " have
washed their robes and made them white in the
blood of the Lamb."

Who are among these last named? Think a
moment. Look back over life and see in imagination the faces of friends once loved, who broke
away from us, and disappeared from view, and
now are " before the throne." Some of these
were of our own households. Some whose vacant
chairs are but sad reminders of them, " absent
from the body, but now present with the Lord."

Where are they? " Before the throne of God,"
in His presence in intimate association with their
Redeemer, in heaven itself, where " they serve him
day and night." Their faces peer at us over the
walls of the Celestial City, their eyes look at us in
imagination as we gaze heavenward, and their
hands beckon us on in our heavenward journey.

Shall we ever see them again? Yes, if faithful
amid tribulation, and if our robes are washed in
the blood of the Lamb.

Will we know them in that unseen land of light and liberty and fulness of joy? By every token. For if Moses and Elijah were recognized on the Mount of Transfiguration; if Stephen knew his Lord as they were stoning him; if Dives in hell recognized Lazarus and Abraham though far off in heaven; if we do not lose our identity in heaven; and are in heaven the same identical persons we were here in this world; with the same peculiarities, the same specific make-up in our entire moral being; if memory holds its sway and performs its functions; then there need be no doubt whatever that we shall know one another in that land, where there is no death, neither sorrow nor crying, neither any more pain, nor separations, " for the former things are passed away."

O, the blessed hope of a glad reunion with departed saints in the glory world! How they do attract us when we look that way!

What vision of glory! What ecstasy came to the Apostle Paul, this saintly man, from his association with Jesus Christ!

Almost unnumbered are the illustrations of a truth so resonant of grace that Jesus Christ, even in this life, is the greatest treasure, the profoundest joy, the most gracious influence that can come to man.

What earthly good can give joy like this? Death robs of every crown of joy but this! Gold, fame, honor, empire, earthly success, all are silenced in the presence of death, which robs of all, separates from all! Jesus Christ only can give triumph over death. He holds the keys of death. Joy in Jesus Christ is unwithered by death's touch.

Come, let us anew Our journey pursue,
    With vigor arise,
And press to our permanent place in the skies:
Of heavenly birth, Though wand'ring on earth,
    This is not the place,
But strangers and pilgrims ourselves we confess.

At Jesus's call We gave up our all;
    And still we forego,
For Jesus's sake, our enjoyments below:
No longing we find For the country behind;
    But onward we move,
And still we are seeking a country above.
                                    —*Charles Wesley.*